1,000
Mitzvahs

1,000 MITZVAHS

--- .... ---

HOW SMALL ACTS
OF KINDNESS CAN
HEAL, INSPIRE, AND
CHANGE YOUR LIFE

--- .... ---

· LINDA COHEN ·

SEAL PRESS

1,000 Mitzvahs
How Small Acts of Kindness Can Heal, Inspire, and Change Your Life
Copyright © 2011 by Linda Cohen

Published by
Seal Press
A Member of the Perseus Books Group
1700 Fourth Street
Berkeley, California

Library of Congress Cataloging-in-Publication Data

Cohen, Linda, 1968-
  1,000 mitzvahs : how small acts of kindness can heal, inspire, and change your life / by
Linda Cohen.
    p. cm.
  ISBN 978-1-58005-365-5
  1. Kindness--Religious aspects--Judaism. 2. Jewish ethics. 3. Jewish way of life. 4.
Cohen, Linda, 1968- 5. Cohen, Linda, 1968---Family. I. Title.
  BJ1286.K5C64 2011
  296.3'677--dc22

                                                                    2010053368

9 8 7 6 5 4 3 2 1

Cover design by Gopa & Ted2
Interior design by www.meganjonesdesign.com

Printed in the United States of America
Distributed by Publishers Group West

In the dark of morn
the light shines through the trees
and reminds me of him.

APRIL 2007

— — — • • • • — — —

In loving memory of my father, Peter Rabow

(MARCH 23, 1936–DECEMBER 1, 2006)

— — — • • • • — — —

"May God remember the soul of my
beloved father who has gone to his eternal
rest. In tribute to his memory I pledge to
perform acts of charity and goodness. May
the deeds I perform and the prayers I offer
help to keep his soul bound up in the bond
of life as an enduring blessing. Amen."

YIZKOR, MEMORIAL SERVICE

CONTENTS

••••

Introduction

I N December 2006, my father, Peter Rabow, died after an eight-month battle with lung cancer. The experience of losing a parent was deeply significant, and it affected my life on nearly every level. My busy life as a mother, wife, and entrepreneur came to a screeching halt. My body and mind felt numb. I had no choice but to take time to contemplate the matters of life and death during what I would later call my "spiritual sabbatical."

Prior to my father's death, he and I had discussed the idea of the mitzvah of *tzedakah*, or donating money in his memory to a charity. We'd played it out rather thoroughly, him suggesting that friends and family not send flowers but rather make donations to "venues that aid people to be the best they can be and help them grow." I'd suggested an organization I knew of, and he told me about ones he'd had in mind. In his obituary, my family requested that friends donate to these charities.

Perhaps the seeds of that conversation sparked the simple thought that awoke me in the middle of the night about a month after my father's death. As I contemplated how meaningful it was that people had donated in the name of my father, in essence allowing his generous spirit to live on, I was inspired to begin a mitzvah project of my own to honor my father's memory. The idea was to perform 1,000 mitzvahs. Mitzvahs are statements and principles of Jewish law and ethics contained in the Torah, or Five Books of Moses. The word mitzvah is translated as commandments. There are 613 mitzvahs. Judaism teaches that Jews are commanded to observe these mitzvahs. There are two types:

Positive commandments are commandments to do something, such as, "honor your mother and father"; and negative commandments are commandments *not* to do something, such as, "thou shalt not murder."

According to Chassidic teachings, the word *mitzvah* is derived from the Hebrew root *tzavta,* meaning "attachment." When we act on a mitzvah, we are creating a bond or a further attachment in our relationship with God. Another rabbi I know teaches his bar and bat mitzvah students that these commandments are "spiritual opportunities" for connection. We create or tap into a connection with God, each other, ourselves, and our history when we engage in a mitzvah.

Many of the 613 mitzvahs can't be observed today for a variety of reasons. Some relate only to the ancient holy Temple in Israel, and they include sacrifices and service. Since the Temple doesn't exist anymore, they can't be observed. Others relate to civil procedures in Israel, and because Israel is a democracy today and is no longer governed directly by religious laws, they are also no longer valid.

An important mitzvah category is doing acts of loving kindness, also called *gemilut chasadim.* The Talmud, a central Jewish text, says that *gemilut chasadim* is greater than *tzedakah* (charity), because unlike *tzedakah, gemilut chasadim* can be done for both the rich and poor, both the living and the dead, and can be done with our actions or with money. "The world is built with kindness" (Psalm 89:3).

People in recent times have begun to use the word *mitzvah* interchangeably with doing an act of kindness because so many of the mitzvahs call upon our deep capacity for true kindness in the world. For my project and this book, that is the way I chose to interpret it, as well.

My intention from the beginning was to use this concept of doing good deeds as a way to honor my father's memory. It felt like a proactive way to work through the pain and loss that I felt in my father's absence. I figured the project would allow me to help others in small ways and create good feelings to compensate for the pangs of grief and sadness.

The next morning, I shared my idea with my husband, a software engineer, who suggested we create a blog to track my mitzvah project. On January 17, 2007, I posted my first blog entry to www.1000mitzvahs .org. I made a conscious decision to use the more Americanized word *mitzvah*, rather than the grammatically correct Hebrew plural *mitzvot*. Although this project is firmly rooted in my religious beliefs, it soon became apparent that it could and would be equally relevant and inspiring to all people. Throughout the project and book, I have continued to use the Americanized word *mitzvahs*, which I originally chose for my blog name.

The night after creating my blog and writing my first entry, I emailed several close friends to tell them about my project. I was nervous about what they would think. I wasn't accustomed to sharing the details of my personal endeavors online. I worried that someone would call me a braggart. I almost didn't send that email because of fear. The next month, I stood up at my networking group when we introduced ourselves and announced that I was taking a spiritual sabbatical from my business as a direct sales consultant and would be starting a new project: to complete and blog about 1,000 mitzvahs I would be performing in memory of my father. The immediate feedback was encouraging. People applauded my efforts and I began to relax into the new adventure I was on.

Prior to starting my blog, I never considered myself a writer. I had kept journals before but never anything that would be read and shared with others. About a month into the project, I received an email from a gentleman in Israel. His one simple comment made a light bulb go off in my head. I recognized that strangers could find my blog and were starting to follow what I was writing. That realization clarified for me that I was not the only one being inspired by this project. I was part of a greater world where one's actions affect others. In fact, each of us is part of this world where our actions of loving kindness effect others. As the months went by, I befriended men and women across the country who found my project and wrote to me. This recognition helped me gain confidence and belief that this project was something that transcended myself, my family, and my religion, and was something I must continue to share and explore further.

THE BLOG WAS an incredible tool for me. It allowed me an opportunity to share my thoughts and feelings as I moved through my grief in a very concrete way. Between the mitzvahs themselves and blogging about the actions, I stumbled onto a powerful combination for processing grief. The mitzvah project did help me remain connected to my father. I felt a deep knowing that my dad and I were on this journey together somehow. The project allowed me to think about him a great deal and to share stories about him, as well.

I began to think of the journey of loss and grief as a trip across a raging river. When you begin the journey of processing grief, you suddenly realize there is no getting around it. It has to be embraced, digested and pondered, and ultimately passed through. When I began trying to cross the river of grief, I felt as if the cold water of the river was rushing over me. I felt alive and aware but also exposed, raw, and numb. Others reached out to me to extend a hand and help me cross the river. I heard stories of others and their own losses. It was comforting when I wondered how long I would feel this way and if I would ever feel "back to normal." While crossing the river, I met others who were crossing their own river of grief. We shared an experience of loss, but each one of us was ultimately on our own to cross that river. I embraced as many hands as I could and took that support while I was in the water. There were moments of normalcy, when I stopped on a rock protruding out of the water, and other times when I slipped back into the cold wetness. Slowly, I made progress crossing the river. Eventually, I offered my hand to someone who was still in the river and encouraged them to keep crossing. There were always people on both sides of the river, everyone helping each other get across.

At some point I reached the other side of the river. I don't remember exactly when it was, but I felt that my feet were fully grounded again on the land and I was no longer actually struggling in the water. Everyone experiences grief in their own way. While I thought at the time that I would always know what to do to help another in their time of grief, the truth is that you really only know about your own experience with grief, and your experience will be uniquely yours. Everyone will take the journey through grief at their own pace and with their own ups and downs. No matter what it looks like, grief can also teach us something about ourselves and our resilience.

After the loss of my dad, it became apparent to me how hard it is to know what action to take to help another person who is going through the grieving process. Each life and death is unique, and not everyone wants the same thing after a death. I have had acquaintances who have lost husbands, brothers, mothers, and fathers, and it is not always clear what to do. Sometimes, religion dictates. If they observe traditional Jewish rituals, perhaps it is easier for me to know what to do, but if they aren't there may not be the same clarity of actions. At the very least, send a sympathy card. Making a meal can also be beneficial. Help organize friends and family to cook for a friend in need.

Whatever you choose to do, acknowledge that someone has had a loss and reach out to your friend or acquaintance even if you aren't sure what to say or do. No one really is.

WHEN I BEGAN my blog and mitzvah project in early 2007, my son was in kindergarten and my daughter was in third grade. At the completion of the project, they were in the second and fifth grades, respectively. In January 2008, one year after beginning the blog, I had officially recorded 550 mitzvahs. By the time I'd been doing mitzvahs for a year, there was no denying that what had started out as a small idea had become something incredibly important in my day-to-day life. After the first year, I had no intention of stopping and was more committed than ever to reach my goal of 1,000 mitzvahs.

I completed the mitzvah project in May 2009, nearly two and a half years after I began. On a friend's suggestion, I organized a final 1,000th mitzvah celebration at a food bank and asked others to help me collect one thousand bags of food. A local columnist wrote an article about me and my project that ran in the Sunday edition of the *Oregonian*. It was a wonderful celebration that brought in more than two thousand pounds of food for the food bank.

During my two and a half years of performing mitzvahs, I discovered that, aside from the moral virtue of doing kind acts, being kind is good for your health and happiness. The giver of kindness receives as much benefit or more than the recipient. I learned firsthand that it truly is better to give than to receive. From the beginning, most of my mitzvahs were simple and duplicable. I didn't set out to save the world. I don't even profess that any of my 1,000 small actions stand out as particularly important or life-changing. But I will assert that each of them made a small impact, and that cumulatively they have changed my life. As a busy wife and mother of two, I found ways to juggle my responsibilities to my family and perform these simple mitzvahs. I also learned that many mitzvahs don't take much time or money.

My hope is that others will copy my idea. Ideas are meant to be shared, and it would give me no greater pleasure than to know that someone else has benefited from my story. This mitzvah project taught me the key to living well: Be in service and give of yourself. I believe that there is no better way to learn, grow, and perhaps to move through a dark time of loss, than to give of yourself with time and effort, and sometimes money. I also hope that classes, groups, and organizations might consider using my ideas or share them with their members. A project like this can certainly benefit the collective, too.

When this idea was nothing more than a what-if, just six weeks after my father died, I had no idea the immense benefits and life-changing experiences that would come about as a result of it. It has, indeed, changed the course of my life, and for that and all the other incredible lessons I have learned along the way, I am especially grateful.

CHAPTER 1

····

FOOD FOR THE BODY, NOURISHMENT FOR THE SOUL

····

"If you can't feed a hundred people, then just feed one."

—MOTHER TERESA

· *food* ·

IN JUDAISM, THERE is a customary meal held on funeral days for the family of the deceased. Mourners gather at the synagogue after they return from the cemetery and share a meal of recovery or condolence. This meal is usually provided by friends, extended family, or community members. In addition to bagels and bread, hard-boiled eggs are often served because their roundness symbolizes the cycle of life. Many communities still observe this tradition, and my father's community was one of them. At a time of deep sorrow and vulnerability, my family was cared for. The meal—the entire experience—reflected the empathy and generosity that thrives in my father's community, and it reminded me of just how much we all depend on others to nurture us through difficult transitions.

While many of the Jewish laws of mourning are followed less and less frequently by nonobservant Jews, they provide a supportive structure that helps mourners move through grief. After losing my father, these mourning rituals were vital to my physical, emotional, and spiritual recovery.

IN MY HOME growing up, food was something more than mere sustenance: It was love. It united our family. In addition to our quiet, intimate family dinners, we often hosted large outdoor parties. For months beforehand, I would eagerly anticipate our annual Labor Day party, which usually drew nearly one hundred guests. My parents would cook for weeks in advance, creating dish after delectable dish. On the day of the party, huge tents would be hoisted outside, shading beautifully arranged picnic tables overflowing with food. Everyone would spend hours eating, laughing, and sharing stories. It is one of my fondest childhood memories. Our family home was also the central location for festive annual Thanksgiving dinners, which often included two dozen or more family guests. Everyone would arrive the Wednesday before Thanksgiving, kicking off a nonstop smorgasbord of food and fun. We'd spend hours playing charades, laughing good-naturedly as older relatives helped younger ones act out their turns. In the evenings, we would warm ourselves by the woodstove and talk for hours. After the Thanksgiving dinner was over, we'd immediately begin making turkey soup for the next night's main course.

I suppose eating and cooking is in my genes. My father adored food and loved to cook; my paternal grandmother, Rosa Rabow, was a kosher caterer in New York City in the 1950s and '60s. I learned early in my life that there's more to serving a meal than simply providing food; it's also about presentation. So much so, that during my father's funeral, a neighbor and I laughed that my dad would likely have commented that doilies were missing from beneath some of the food arrangements. Cooking was an art, but also something that tied us together. The memories of my father are indelibly linked to memories of food—the smells, the tastes, the rituals of preparing and eating meals together, the intimacy it engendered, and the stories surrounding it.

For example, I'll never forget the time I decided to keep kosher. I was fifteen. In its simplest terms, keeping kosher means eating only certain meats slaughtered in a specific manner, not mixing any meat and dairy products, and refraining from pork and shellfish altogether. Importing kosher meat into our rural community in Vermont was a challenge, to say the least. My father and stepmother didn't greet the decision with enthusiasm. Our home was not kosher; in fact, we'd actually raised and slaughtered pigs for food. I had enjoyed bacon and ham from pigs that we'd raised lovingly, fed from our kitchen scraps. My decision to keep kosher drastically shifted what I deemed "acceptable food options." My father was bothered by the inconvenience and promptly told me that my teenage "kosher phase" probably wouldn't last. Alas, it lasted into my forties.

I shudder when I think about the fact that an estimated thirty-seven million Americans don't have enough food to eat. For so many of us, it is something that nourishes us beyond mere physical needs, but at its most basic, food is necessary for our survival, and too many people just don't have enough. Despite these seemingly insurmountable numbers, there are thousands of food programs working to help eradicate hunger across the country. During my two years of doing mitzvahs, I learned about food pantries, projects to help feed homeless people in the parks, and many other volunteer programs that ensure food gets delivered to those in need. There are so many different kinds of organizations out there battling hunger in America, but they share one thing in common: They need our help. They need our dollars as well as our time. This chapter showcases some of the small things I did during the mitzvah project, but they only scratch the surface of the many ways that each of us can help. Food-related mitzvahs help feed people, and they also nourish souls.

Give a Lunch and Get Inspired

A MONTH AFTER my father died, I learned that the celebrated children's book author and storyteller Eric Kimmel was invited to my daughter's school as an author-in-residence. I frequently volunteer at the school for field trips, assemblies, and other special events, so when the coordinator learned how excited I was by his visit, she asked if I wouldn't mind picking up lunch for him. I was more than happy to help.

Eric Kimmel turned out to be an amazing speaker. Even my preschool-age son, whom I'd brought along for the adventure, was delighted. Kimmel's insight, experience, and giving nature provided an example to the children that they could share their ideas, thoughts, and imagination with the world if they so desired. After his reading, Kimmel signed two books we already owned for my son. But I was so taken by the spirit of his work and his generosity that I purchased a copy of *The Magic Dreidels* and had him sign it for my daughter, plus I bought an additional copy for my son's school. At the end of the day we left with four signed books and a wealth of inspiration.

• • • •

THIS MITZVAH STARTED out as an opportunity to provide lunch to someone who was doing a service for my daughter's school, but I walked away with so much more than I had given. In this case, I'd provided a store-bought sandwich for our speaker, and in return I received a day's worth of inspiration. Looking back, perhaps listening to him that day inspired me to become an author, as well.

♥ *Volunteer in the school cafeteria, bring in food for the teachers, organize other parents to bring in food for a class activity, or pick up food for an upcoming PTO meeting.*

Give Thanks for the Small Things

EVEN SMALL THINGS can have a big impact. I purchased some fish for dinner one day that turned out to be so delicious that I returned to our local market the next morning to thank the man who prepared it for us. It was halibut coated in bread crumbs, Parmesan, and seasoning—and it was scrumptious. He'd even gone out of his way to explain how to cook it properly. As I waited at the counter for him, I was still thinking how good the meal had turned out and how easy it had been to prepare. I thought about how thanking someone for doing their job well is encouraging. It confirms to them that their time and effort helped someone else. When he arrived at the counter, I told him the food was a big hit and easy to prepare, and I thanked him for it. He was quite pleased. He smiled and told me he was just doing his job, but I couldn't help but notice the gleam in his eye!

• • • •

THIS IS THE simplest of mitzvahs: going out of your way to thank someone for the role they played in your well-being. And yet, what is easy to do is also easy *not* to do. The response I got from the man at the fish market taught me that thanking another human being can really make a difference in their day. We often spend so much time complaining and griping about the things that aren't working for us in our day-to-day lives that we rarely stop to acknowledge those things that *are* working. Doing so is not only good for the recipient, it's also good for us. This simple exchange filled me with goodwill and a sense of kinship. Giving gratitude can change the world. This is a mitzvah that each of us is capable of doing every single day.

♥ *Take time to give thanks to someone, whether a friend or a stranger.*

Make a Meal for a Person in Need

WHEN SOMEONE IS going through a difficult time, providing them with a meal can help more than we realize. When a friend of mine had a relatively simple surgery, it offered the opportunity to put a simple action into play, with positive results. Although my friend wasn't confined to a bed, she was overburdened by the daily needs of her home and family when instead she needed to be resting. I made her a pot of vegetable soup, a salad, and bread from my bread machine, yet her gratefulness belied the meal's simplicity. Of course, my kids were irritated because the act of delivering the food had postponed their own snack time. The irony was not lost on me.

• • • •

HELPING A FRIEND in need is easier than you might think, and it doesn't have to be a big production. Once, a friend of mine whose husband had been in the hospital for an extended period of time asked if I would make some muffins for the nurses who had been so attentive to him. It was easy enough, and she was grateful. But not all people experiencing hardship will reach out in this way, and not simply because of pride. They're worried that by asking for help they will be a burden to you. Sometimes, when you know someone is in need but they resist soliciting help, a little gentle probing may uncover ways you can assist them. The meals I've received from friends during trying times in my life have been a wonderful gift, and they've enhanced our connections. You might consider making meals for someone who's just had a baby, is recovering after a hospital stay, or is grieving after the loss of a person, pet, relationship, or job.

And remember, you certainly don't have to be a gourmet cook. A simple meal is fine! If the person I am cooking for has children, I might

FOOD FOR THE BODY, NOURISHMENT FOR THE SOUL

15

make lasagna, homemade mac-n-cheese, or a pot of soup and a loaf of bread from our bread machine. It is a nourishing gesture of kindness.

♥ *Who do you know that might need a comforting meal? Keep this idea in mind next time one of your friends or a community member is sick or going through a rough time.*

MITZVAH 583

Acknowledge Actions with Kind Words

ONE DAY WHEN my kids and I were at the supermarket, they noticed there was a mess of spilled coffee beans and grounds around the coffee grinder. They brushed the grounds into their hands and threw them into the trash—without me asking them to! An employee noticed their good deed and thanked them for their help. I was quick to affirm my kids' thoughtful gesture and thanked them for taking it upon themselves to offer their assistance.

• • • •

OKAY, SO THIS was really my kids' mitzvah, but it was important to me because it confirmed that all my own mitzvah-doing was setting a good example and encouraging my kids to be active helpers in the world. When the supermarket employee thanked my children for helping him out, I was also grateful for his acknowledgment. Would I have praised their helpful action if he hadn't noticed it first? I wondered. How often had I reprimanded my kids in those same supermarket aisles for pulling things off the shelf or begging me to buy items we didn't need? Our kids need to be praised for the good they're doing, and being recognized by a stranger can hold a lot of value. Here was my chance to actually give them positive feedback for their actions. Recently, I had the opportunity to do the same for someone else. I told a friend about something positive I witnessed her preteen daughter doing. My friend was thrilled to hear it, and I imagine she, in turn, praised her daughter. The goodness that comes from positive reinforcement can be powerful.

♥ *You can be that praising stranger. Pay attention to the positive actions of others and be sure to share your observation and acknowledge their good deeds.*

Volunteer for a Community Fundraiser

EVERY SPRING, ONE of the most festive of all Jewish holidays, Purim, is celebrated. This annual festival commemorates the freeing of the Jewish people from the Persian nobleman Haman and his plot to destroy them, as recorded in the Book of Esther. Traditionally, revelers dress in masks and costumes, give out gifts of food, provide charity to the less fortunate, and enjoy a celebratory dinner, the Feast of Purim. One long-standing tradition is baking and giving out gifts of fruit-filled, triangular cookies called *Hamantaschen* (Yiddish for "Haman's pockets"). The dough is rolled out, cut into circles, and filled with a poppy seed or prune filling, and then wrapped into a triangular shape. For more than thirty years, men and women in my synagogue have gathered to make, bake, and sell these cookies as a fundraiser. Community members volunteer significant amounts of time and ingredients to produce the cookies. It is such a joyous and unifying community event, it's easy to forget how labor-intensive it is! But it's worth it. I hadn't volunteered to help with the cookies for several years, so I was excited to join the group. It was hard work, but it was also wonderful and fulfilling to be part of my community and create something that would earn money for our synagogue. Working together, we baked batch after batch of cookies, and when I picked my kids up after school with cookies in hand, they were delighted! My daughter asked if the ones I'd brought were the ones I'd actually made myself. Of course, I had no idea, but I didn't have the heart to tell her. I think it was enough that every cookie, whether made by me or someone else in my community, was made with the same love and generosity of spirit. The cookie-making lasted three weeks, so I was able to take my daughter back another day to experience it herself. She did so well, some of the older women told her she even shaped the cookies better than I did. She loved that!

• • • •

FOR ME, THIS event, like so many others, is steeped in nostalgia. Think bake sales, lemonade stands, spaghetti dinners, strawberry shortcake festivals, and *Hamantaschen* baking. People coming together to cook, share, and raise money. These simple food-oriented gatherings provide a great backdrop for connecting with people in our communities and giving back to others. I hadn't attended these cookie-making events in years because the daily responsibilities of life and family demanded my time. Choosing to participate that year turned out to be a refreshing and important reminder of the camaraderie of community. It was made even more meaningful by my daughter's delight in being a part of it and earning the praise of community members. She was thrilled to be told her cookies were prettier than mine. So was I.

By immersing myself in something that is both traditional and community-building, I was brought back to my roots—and it was a delicious mitzvah to boot.

♥ *Volunteer your time at a food-related community event. Help ensure that these timeless gatherings continue into the next generation.*

Contribute to a Food Drive

MY SON CAME home one day and announced that his school was participating in a project for the local food bank. He informed me that they were to gather up canned food and bring it to school the next day. *Wonderful!* I thought. *He's really drawn to helping others. My own mitzvahs are really setting a good example!* I dove right in, reiterating to him the importance of helping others and telling him how great I thought it was that he was participating in a project that directed food to people in need. He said: "Well, the teacher said we *had* to do it." So much for patting myself on the back! Regardless, we gathered up a bagful of food, and he ended up feeling pretty happy about carrying it into class the next day.

• • • •

SOMETIMES DOING A mitzvah just because the teacher told us to is good enough. It's certainly better than giving begrudgingly or not giving at all. My son hadn't been the one to suggest the idea of contributing to the food bank. So what? Most of us give in response to things that people ask us to do. Whether you give time or money or canned goods, responding to someone's call for assistance is an opportunity to do good in your community and help others. The holidays offer countless opportunities for such charity, but there are year-round opportunities to be generous and giving, as well. Most schools, grocery stores, and offices gather food and toys for kids on a regular basis. If you hear of a food or clothing drive, consider that even a single item can make a difference in a less-fortunate person's life. When I saw my son proudly carrying his bag of food to class that day, I knew that his sense that this was nothing more than just another school requirement had flown out the window.

This experience reminded me of Maimonides, a twelfth-century Jewish scholar who invented the Eight Levels of giving. Each rung represents a higher degree of virtue. Here are the levels, with 1 being the lowest and 8 being the highest:

1. Giving begrudgingly and making the recipient feel disgraced or embarrassed.

2. Giving cheerfully but giving too little.

3. Giving cheerfully and adequately but only after being asked.

4. Giving before being asked.

5. Giving when you do not know who is the individual benefiting, but the recipient knows your identity.

6. Giving when you know who is the individual benefiting, but the recipient does not know your identity.

7. Giving when neither the donor nor the recipient is aware of the other's identity.

8. Giving money, a loan, your time, or whatever else it takes to enable an individual to be self-reliant.

♥ *Give at Maimonides' fourth level of giving: giving cheerfully before being asked. Take cans of fruits, vegetables, peanut butter, or pasta to a food pantry.*

Ding Dong! Collect for a Food Bank

OUR SYNAGOGUE WAS participating in an annual food drive. My children grudgingly agreed to help but told me they weren't going to ring anyone's doorbell or ask for handouts. However, when we stopped at the first house, the home owner was friendly and warm. He put my kids at ease by asking questions about what we were doing and how the donated food would be used. My son answered him enthusiastically, and I was thrilled that this gentleman had bothered to take the time to engage my kids and get them excited about the impact the food drive would have on others. From that point on, the kids ran from house to house, racing to see who could ring the next doorbell and explain our mission. When we finished, my ten-year-old daughter sheepishly commented, "It was surprisingly fun," and my son, who ended up being first at the front doors most often, eagerly agreed.

• • • •

LIKE MOST KIDS, mine were less than thrilled about the idea of participating in mitzvah activities they thought would be boring or embarrassing. But as it turned out, we were all surprised to find that filling an empty wagon with donated cans and boxes of food would actually be exhilarating. That night, both kids eagerly shared stories and bragged about all the food they had collected. To them, it was similar to trick-or-treating, but instead of hoarding bags of candy for themselves, they were collecting food for the hungry. This door-to-door collecting activity also provided opportunities for the children to engage with people in the community. At the end of the day, our whole family was surprised by how this day turned out.

Sometimes, a little encouragement or positive feedback will help children get involved, especially when the volunteer activity sounds more like work than play. They might even surprise themselves by how much they enjoy it.

♥ *Stop at the grocery store with your children and have them choose three items to donate to a food pantry. Many stores have collection bins at the front of the store.*

Dine at a Philanthropic Restaurant

ON OCCASION, RESTAURANTS will donate a portion of their day's proceeds to a charitable cause. When I learned that several of my local neighborhood restaurants had joined together to donate one night's proceeds to the Oregon Food Bank (OFB), my family decided it was the perfect reason to dine out. That afternoon, we ran into some friends at the gym and I invited them to join us. What a great opportunity to socialize *and* raise money for a good cause. Suddenly a lightbulb went off! Why not tell others? The more people who ate out, the more money could be raised for OFB. I called a few other families and invited them to eat out, too.

• • • •

THIS MITZVAH STARTED with a specific goal—to eat at a restaurant that was giving back; however, it turned into so much more when I realized I could spread the word. If you are engaged in a mitzvah or good deed and you can encourage others to join you, do it! You can invite a child, spouse, parent, friend, or colleague. It's simply a matter of asking people to participate. There is nothing to lose and so much to gain. Sharing the opportunity to give is even more enjoyable when done with others.

♥ *Invite a friend to join you at a charitable dinner or event.*

Volunteer to Deliver Perishable Foods

THROUGHOUT THE SCHOOL year, Metro Portland runs Fork It Over, a food donation program to reduce hunger and waste in the Portland metropolitan area. This is a great program since it makes use of perishable items that would otherwise go to waste. My job was to pick up leftover food from a local elementary school's cafeteria and deliver it to the food pantry. Instead of perishable items from the schools going to waste over spring break, the school district donated them to the local food pantry. Dozens of schools participated. In addition, hundreds of local restaurants, caterers, and food service companies regularly fight hunger and reduce waste by donating to Fork It Over! Similar programs exist throughout the United States, and the volunteer jobs are generally easy to do and easy to fit into your schedule. So much so, that I even nicknamed it the "lunchtime mitzvah" since it can be done in less than an hour.

• • • •

THROUGHOUT THIS PROJECT, I became more aware of the numerous opportunities to deliver and provide food to local pantries. These are important services, and good food shouldn't be thrown away! In order to participate, many organizations, restaurants, and programs depend on volunteers to make the deliveries. It is a quick and nearly effortless way to help ensure that food doesn't get wasted and instead gets to those who really need it.

♥ *Find out if your school district donates leftover food to a local food pantry, then sign up to help.*

Initiate a Food Drive

IN HONOR OF my dad, who loved to cook, my 1,000th mitzvah had to be related to food. To this day, my favorite breakfast is still a steaming bowl of Cream of Wheat filled to the brim with milk and raisins, which my father served to me on cold, snowy Vermont mornings. When I got married, my father and stepmother's gift to us was a three-ring fabric binder filled with all their favorite recipes—their own and their friends'. That cookbook has become a precious keepsake. For years now, I have made my father's chicken piccata, which requires just five ingredients— easy and delicious.

My 1,000th mitzvah was inspired by the tough economic times that had been plaguing our country. I decided to use the enormity of my final mitzvah to make a request—that all my readers give food or money to their local Jewish Family Services, food bank, shelter, or friend in need. One dollar is equivalent to five pounds of food, and there are many great programs that can transfer your money into sustainable meals for people in need.

• • • •

NOT ALL OF us have a platform to ask others to help. It's true that I decided to make my last mitzvah about putting out the call for help. This resulted in a 1,000th Mitzvah Celebration at the Sunshine Pantry. It was a fabulous success. So many of us can do this in our own small ways. Never underestimate what you can do. With the help of others, anything is possible.

♥ *Gather your friends and family and volunteer at your local shelter, as a group, to serve meals.*

CHAPTER 2

....

CHANGE THE TOILET PAPER

....

"We can ask ourselves daily what we have done to make the world a better place, to make someone smile, to help someone to feel more secure, etc. It's the simple things which have the greatest effect. We must never underestimate the strength of a smile or act of kindness."

—DR. LEO BUSCAGLIA

· paying it forward ·

I N THE 1970s, my father and stepmother fled the big city to live a
more rural life in Vermont. They bought an old farmhouse with a
large plot of land. There was quite a learning curve to living in a
rural community, but they thrived. I moved in with them when I was
a teenager and soon found out that Vermonters live by the Golden
Rule: "Do unto your neighbors as you would have them do unto you."
Together, folks in the community farmed, made maple sugar, and
pressed cider. People knew their neighbors and watched out for each
other. It didn't have to be taught; it was how things were.

When my father and stepmother moved to Burlington, Vermont
in the 1990s, they joined a special community dubbed the Wednesday
Morning Group. They met every Wednesday at his synagogue. It wasn't
a religious group, and many of the members weren't even Jewish, but
the synagogue provided a space to meet. Each Wednesday this group,
comprised of men and women who were brought together by shared
interests, spent an hour and a half talking, sharing, and experiencing
life. Afterward, many of them went out to breakfast together.

My father had been part of this group for over ten years when he
found out he had terminal cancer. The members of the group, which
he now counted among his most intimate friends, prayed for him and
encouraged and sustained him when he discovered he was dying. I
remember a conversation I had with my father during the last three
weeks of his life. He had attended what he imagined would be his last
Wednesday Morning Group that day. He told me how each of the group
members had hugged him and whispered to him how much they loved
him. He was content yet sad to be leaving this unbelievably special
group of people.

I was with my father the week he died. I arrived in Vermont on a
Saturday and went straight to his home. He was resting peacefully, but I

was bracing myself for the inevitable. For several days, my family spent time sitting with my father, and it was very difficult to see him this way. That week, my stepmother encouraged me to attend the Wednesday Morning Group. These complete strangers, who had known and loved my father so deeply, held me as I gave in to my sorrow, which seemed so intractable at the time. Watching him lying in bed, waiting for the inevitable end, was too much to bear. A part of me wanted his death to come soon, if only to shorten my suffering. (He wasn't really suffering, but as his daughter it was difficult to see this vibrant man in such a reduced state.)

The group encouraged me to surrender to the unknown and find solace in knowing my father's death would come when he was ready. My thoughts about death and loss will forever be shifted because of those men and women. Having someone to talk to, to help me embrace the shift from resistance to acceptance, gave me a profound sense of comfort in the midst of my despair.

Since my father's death, I have tried to offer solace to both friends and strangers when they are grieving. This might mean comforting someone who has experienced a loss, being there for someone who is going through a hard time, or engaging in any number of small actions that can have a positive impact on others. Now that I live in Portland, Oregon, I'm nostalgic for that small-town culture I grew up with in Vermont, but this mitzvah project allowed me to re-create that feeling everywhere I went.

♥ *Keep your eyes open and be aware of what your neighbors, friends, and strangers are going through. It's an opportunity to pay it forward in your daily life.*

Compliment a Dedicated Employee

WE WERE ON a family trip when I spilled tea on the white sweater I was wearing. I was upset and it was affecting my mood. When we got to the hotel where we were staying, I asked one of the housekeeping staff if she had any dish soap so that I could do a fast fix in the room. She didn't. Not five minutes later, there was a knock at our door. It was the woman again, this time with dish soap in hand. I was grateful and let her know as much, thanking her for going out of her way to help me. I called the manager of the hotel and told him about her quick and thoughtful gesture. He appreciated the call and the acknowledgment of great customer service. He promised he'd pass on the compliment.

• • • •

WHEN WE ARE displeased with service we get as customers, patrons, or guests, we are so eager to share our negative feedback. We report or complain about the situation and want justice served pronto. But how often do we report someone's superior customer service? Through her speedy actions, this hotel employee showed compassion and understanding and all but altered my deteriorating mood. That's worth a lot. I wanted her boss to know.

Every day, we have interactions with people doing their jobs well. Acknowledging their conscientious behavior is not only kind, but it also serves to reinforce their high-standard performance.

♥ *Tell a manager about an employee's exemplary customer service.*

Change the Toilet Paper!

WHILE TRAVELING IN Spain with my husband, I visited a bathroom stall with no toilet paper. Luckily, I had some Kleenex in my purse, but I decided not to leave the next person in the same position. I found a roll in the bathroom and put it in the stall. A small kindness for a stranger....

• • • •

WELL, THIS SMALL mitzvah elicited quite a big discussion between me and my husband. How could a simple gesture like changing the toilet paper evoke such a lively conversation about trust and vulnerability? If you've ever seen the hilarious, now-famous *Seinfeld* episode in which Elaine asks another bathroom patron, "Can you spare a square?" you'll know *exactly* what I'm talking about. I, too, once found myself in the position of having to ask a stranger to "spare a square" for me. Luckily she did. That's trust and vulnerability in a nutshell.

Did this mitzvah count as an act of kindness for a stranger? We determined that it did.

Making sure to never leave a stranger in this "exposed" position is a thoughtful display of kindness. When you change the toilet paper roll, you directly prevent another person from having to experience this extremely vulnerable and helpless situation. If you find yourself swinging open the door to a paper-less stall, be courteous and change the toilet paper roll or notify someone who can.

♥ *Change a roll of toilet paper in the restroom.*

Listen with an Open Heart

ON CHRISTMAS DAY at Disney World, we were stuck in an hour-long line waiting for one of the rides when I struck up a conversation with another woman in line. She also had two kids, and they looked about the same age as mine. After a bit of small talk, she began to share her sad story with me. The summer before, she had lost her older fourteen-year-old son, who had been killed in an accident. This was the family's first Christmas without him. To temper the pain of his absence, they decided to come to Disney World for the holidays, to do something different. I could see what a difficult time this was for her, and I was moved to hug her. She seemed to appreciate being able to talk openly about the tragedy, even though I was a stranger. She mentioned how hard it had been on her younger son, since the two boys had been very close. My heart ached for this mom. When we reached the front of the line, I offered a silent prayer that somehow time would help ease her grief.

• • • •

FOR PARENTS, LOSING a child is the most profound loss there is. Most of us can't even imagine the pain of such a thing, and yet there are many parents who find themselves having to cope with a child's death.

In her well-known book, *On Death and Dying*, Elisabeth Kübler-Ross states that each one of us will move through five stages of grief after any loss. These stages are denial, anger, bargaining, depression, and acceptance. According to this model, grief is grief. Individuals may not go through the stages in the same order—some may last longer than others, or we may get stuck in one stage and not be able to move forward—but each of us will experience grief after a loss.

When I met this stranger in line, I realized we had something in common even though I decided that my grief over losing my father didn't compare to the depth of despair she must have been experiencing over the loss of her son. However, I understood what grief felt like. Our connection was the mutual understanding of death. Confronting death, grief, and loss has fostered a deeper empathy toward others who have experienced loss. It has made me a more sensitive listener. Grief is shared by everyone, no matter our race, religion, culture, or gender. Allowing yourself to be with someone who is experiencing grief and loss can be sad but also incredibly rewarding, for both parties.

♥ *Listen to people you meet with an open and giving heart.*

For Heart: Give Gifts Spontaneously

A FRIEND WHO works for a local nonprofit invited me to their annual luncheon. I attended and was moved to donate to their charity. After the luncheon, my friend encouraged me to take two centerpieces home. As I walked back to my car with flower arrangements in each hand, a young canvasser approached me to solicit money for another nonprofit, an international children's relief organization. I stopped, listened, and chatted with her for several minutes. I chose not to donate, since I was coming from a luncheon where I'd just given money to charity. As I walked away, a thought came to me. I turned back and gave the canvasser one of the centerpieces I was carrying. She was thrilled, and so were her two young associates.

• • • •

I STRUGGLE WHEN a solicitor approaches me on the street. I don't want to be rude, and I know how hard it is to solicit people through calls and in person, let alone on the street. Yet, often this feels like an invasion of my privacy and space. I decided that being polite to this solicitor was already an act of kindness, but giving her flowers and seeing her face light up was even better. Spontaneous giving can be really addictive.

♥ *Try spontaneous giving.*

Give a Stranger a Towel

OUR GYM ENACTED a policy of moving the towels outside of the locker rooms. Apparently, it dropped towel usage by 50 percent. The downside to the new policy is that if you forget to grab a towel before you get into the shower, you'll find yourself in a bit of a predicament! This inevitably happened to me not too far into the new arrangement, and I had to ask someone to get me a towel. I returned the favor a few days later, and several times over, knowing how uncomfortable and awkward it is to find yourself wet, naked, and towel-less. What goes around comes around. It's good to know that the women at the gym have my back and I have theirs.

• • • •

I'M VERY FOND of the mantra, "What goes around comes around." So much so that my kids sometimes roll their eyes when I say it—but it's true. It's the golden rule, and every religion acknowledges it. Do unto others as you would have them do unto you. It doesn't matter if it's a small thing like getting a towel for a naked stranger. As this mitzvah proves, the small things are sometimes the biggest lifesavers.

♥ *The next time you're at the gym, get someone a towel. If towels are plentiful and accessible, clean someone's equipment or put someone's weights away.*

CHANGE THE TOILET PAPER

Help a Fellow Shopper Carry Their Load

ON MY WAY out of Target, I spotted an older couple slowly making their way to the parking lot. The wife was in a wheelchair, and her husband was trying to simultaneously push her down the sidewalk and balance a large box of items they had just purchased. I offered to carry the box to the car while he pushed the wheelchair. They were so grateful, and it made me happy to be able to give them some assistance.

• • • •

IT RARELY REQUIRES heroic action to help a stranger. The simple action of noticing somebody needs assistance, and then stopping and offering to help them, is not that hard. It might mean taking an extra minute or two out of your day, but the reward of providing someone with a little assistance is well worth your time.

Once I was actively engaged in identifying mitzvah possibilities, I found that they were everywhere. Soon after I started the project, a friend told me she offered her cell phone to an elderly woman at church whose husband had yet to arrive to pick her up. The woman was upset and had no way of knowing what had happened to her husband. She called him and discovered that he was fine and just running late. My friend said normally she might not have noticed the woman, but since I had shared my project, she was also looking for ways to assist others.

When you're conscious of your surroundings, you'll notice countless opportunities to help in small ways. I've found that I receive more kindness from strangers, too.

♥ *Assist someone by carrying their groceries or packages.*

Let a Fellow Shopper Go Ahead of You

I WAS IN the checkout line at Trader Joe's unloading my overflowing basket of groceries when a man came up behind me with only one item. I asked if he wanted to go first. He was elated and told me that was the best thing that had happened to him all day. He smiled as he paid the cashier, telling her about my gesture, as well.

• • • •

IT'S THE LITTLE things in life that make us smile. I was amazed that this gentleman would remark that my small courtesy was the nicest thing that had happened to him all day. You never know how your kindness will affect someone. He must have had a pretty lousy day up until that point, because honestly, letting someone go first is no big deal. I'm guessing that my seemingly insignificant action changed all that because he left in such good spirits. Those little actions can change our inner dialogue and affect how we treat others. It's clear that our universe is in dire need of more positive energy. Engaging in spontaneous acts of kindness will work wonders for increasing it.

♥ *Let someone go ahead of you in the checkout line.*

Give Unused Tickets to a Stranger

I WAS DISAPPOINTED when I realized that a lecture I had planned to attend was scheduled on the first night of Passover. I emailed a colleague from my networking group to ask if she knew anyone who'd want to purchase my ticket. I figured if I couldn't attend, at least I could get my money back. Instead, my colleague responded back to me with a request. She had a friend who'd recently finished chemotherapy and couldn't afford to buy a ticket. She asked if I wanted to "do a mitzvah" and pass it on to her friend.

I have to admit, my first thought was not yes. I mulled it over for a moment and remembered all of the gifts I had received from women in my networking group, including support and guidance, flowers, books, a labeler, free tickets, gift certificates, and more. With that, I responded "yes" and gave my ticket to a stranger.

• • • •

LIVING IN GRATITUDE means noticing everything in your life you are grateful for. Sometimes that can be challenging. Returning to that place is often humbling and helpful. Sometimes we need to be reminded to think about the generosity that others have shown us in order to mirror the same altruism.

When I told my kids about giving away my ticket, my son said, "Sometimes there is the easy thing to do and sometimes there is the right thing to do. You chose the right thing." I know he was right!

♥ *Give something to someone today that would benefit them.*

CHAPTER 3

····

VOLUNTEER
WITH A
VENGEANCE

····

*"Everyone has what to give. It can be
something simple like collecting canned
goods. The important thing is to do it.
Don't wait to do a mitzvah tomorrow,
because tomorrow may be too late."*

—RABBANIT BRACHA KAPACH

· *volunteer work* ·

I SPOKE AT a volunteer appreciation dessert for a retirement community in April 2009, a month before I finished my mitzvah project. At the luncheon, the coordinator announced that this group of fifty seniors had given over 22,000 hours of volunteer service over the past year. Impressive! The senior honored as Volunteer of the Year told me, in no uncertain terms, "I hate it when people complain that they're bored or there is nothing to do!" She keeps busy and active with daily volunteer duties that give her great pleasure. She encourages others to give of themselves instead of complaining.

A survey by the U.S. Bureau of Labor Statistics showed that in 2009, about 63.4 million people, or 26.8 percent of the population, volunteered through or for an organization at least once. That number is astoundingly low! One thing this mitzvah project has taught me is that volunteering doesn't have to be hard, or even time-consuming, and if I can have one small lasting impact on people, I hope it's in the area of increased volunteerism. In addition to helping others, you gain a tremendous amount from the experience of volunteering. Those of you who do it regularly can probably attest to how addicting it can be! Sure, you are giving of your time, but the rewards far exceed any amount of time you give.

I haven't always been an active volunteer. I don't have any childhood memories of our family volunteering together. My father participated on the volunteer ski patrol at the ski resort in our town, but it wasn't something we did together as a family.

My first recollection of participating in any kind of organized fundraiser for charity was in junior high when I took part in the Jump Rope for Heart program to raise money for the American Heart Association. This program launched as a national fundraising event in 1978 when I was ten. The students at our school must have been among the first groups of kids to participate in this program, and I remember the experience vividly. We had to collect pledges for donations before the event and there were prizes for all the participants.

Later, in high school, I joined United Synagogue Youth and began to learn about the traditions of giving that are a core tenet of Judaism. I was introduced to the idea of mitzvah heroes, men and women who dedicate themselves to causes they care passionately about—people like Clara Hammer, known as the Chicken Lady of Jerusalem, and Rabbanit Bracha Kapach, who's lived in Jerusalem for forty years and has dedicated herself to all sorts of volunteer projects. She collects used clothing to distribute to those who need it. She has helped provide weddings and bar and bat mitzvah celebrations for people who couldn't afford it, has found people who could donate food and flowers, and has even gotten volunteer musicians and videographers. In addition, she has a famous collection of bridal gowns she lends out to brides. And this doesn't even cover her most famous project, which is collecting and distributing food for Passover. Rabbanit Bracha Kapach has a magnetic personality that attracts volunteers and donors to her, and she and her volunteers distribute thousands of food packages each year, feeding more than 20,000 people. She raises $125,000 annually for this project through private donors. Each of her projects would make her a mitzvah hero, but collectively it is hard to believe what this woman has single-handedly accomplished in her lifetime. Each project she started began with an individual need, and she is an inspiration for all of us.

We are not all destined to become mitzvah heroes, but we can all volunteer in ways that assist and do the important legwork so needed to help people across all walks of life. We can offer our time and energy to programs in our communities that need us to survive.

Even though I learned about volunteering as a teenager, I didn't really delve into it myself on a more consistent basis until my early thirties, after my husband and I relocated to Portland. I was working part-time and had some free time in our new city. It was then that I began volunteering once a week at the local Japanese garden as a tour guide. Around that same time, I started volunteering to answer phones for a fall fund drive for Oregon Public Broadcasting. I also accepted a request to serve on the board of our synagogue. After that, I was hooked on volunteering and have been an active volunteer at several organizations ever since.

If you're not currently volunteering, ask yourself, what's holding you back? Too busy? Every volunteer I know has a full life, too. Careers, kids, aging parents, you name it. And yet many people find time to fit in volunteer hours. Start small. Find an hour a month that you can give and start with that. Flip off the television and replace that time with active volunteer service. I promise it will reward you in spades.

A volunteer position can help you:

- decide on a career.
- make new friends.
- find role models.
- build self-confidence and gain self-esteem.

Maybe you're not sure where to start. Get online and search for organizations in your area that can make use of your talents. If you love animals, type in "animal organizations" and the name of your city. You can do this with anything you might have an interest in. The Internet will help connect you with wonderful new opportunities.

I encourage you to find ways to engage your children in volunteer opportunities, as well. I know firsthand that it's not always easy to get your kids excited about the idea of spending their free time volunteering, but if you can find meaningful and fun opportunities, you can often create positive family volunteer experiences.

Many of the busiest people I know are volunteering small amounts of time and finding that it makes a huge impact on things they care about: our schools, nonprofit organizations, spiritual organizations, and many other worthy causes. Find something you are truly passionate about and go volunteer!

Regardless of what volunteer job you choose to do, you will benefit professionally and personally. You might make contacts that help you with your career. Volunteering looks great on a resume and you'll learn leadership skills and potentially improve your interpersonal or communication skills. On a personal level, it's wonderful to feel needed, appreciated, and valued as a volunteer!

Volunteering for an Organization
That Helps Women in Need

VOLUNTEERING AS A personal shopper for Dress for Success meant helping the women this organization serves find clothes for their upcoming job interviews. One woman was unsure about some of the clothes I'd helped pick out, but she was glowing once she tried them on. She was grateful to have found a fabulous outfit and felt like a million bucks. This is exactly the kind of confidence someone needs when they're going for an interview! At the end of the morning, she thanked me and gave me a hug. Looking at how professional and happy she looked made me feel like a million bucks, too!

• • • •

BEFORE MY CHILDREN were born, we lived close to a beautiful Japanese garden in Portland where I trained to be a docent. I gave tours every week and loved connecting with visitors from all over the world. I continued as a guide for a short while after my daughter was born, taking her around with me in her Baby Bjorn, but that soon got too difficult. After my son was born, I started volunteering at Dress for Success. My mom watched my children one morning a month so I could help the women. The personal interaction with them was gratifying. Now that my children are in school every day, most of my volunteer time revolves around school-related activities. I also serve on the board of directors for their summer arts camp.

Organizations need volunteers. Don't wait to be asked to get involved. Find out who coordinates volunteers and contact them directly. Offer your services for an upcoming event or activity. Be proactive and take the initiative rather than waiting for someone to contact you! If you are passionate about an organization, you'll love playing an important role in its vitality.

♥ *Contact an organization that could use your help and volunteer.*

Volunteering on a Committee

ONCE A MONTH, I volunteered to work at the registration table for my networking meeting. My job was to register attendees, take payments, answer questions, and smile! I loved being able to welcome guests and members to our monthly meeting. Volunteering for the organization helped me keep abreast of important activities in the group. As a working mom, I found that my volunteer job provided a level of value and appreciation that sometimes my role as a mother did not.

• • • •

SEVERAL YEARS AGO, I started my own business doing consulting for a direct sales health and wellness company. I decided it made good business sense for me to join a networking group to meet people and have access to resources and resourceful people. I was quick to volunteer to be on the registration/greeter committee, which involved manning the registration table. This job allowed me to meet all the club members and was a great way to break the ice with other members when I was new. If you aren't an extrovert like me, being a greeter may not appeal to you.

Perhaps you'd rather join a committee to work behind the scenes. There are many kinds of volunteer jobs within a given organization, so the important thing is to take action. In Judaism, there is an important concept called *tikkun olam. Tikkun olam* means "repairing the world." Conceptualized by Rabbi Isaac Luria, a sixteenth-century Kabbalist and Jewish mystic, this interpretation gained traction in the Jewish movements of the 1950s. In its simplest form, *tikkun olam* means to address that which is not working in our world—poverty, hunger, disease—and help to fix it. It stems from the idea that when God created the world, there were divine shards of light that shattered the vessels

He placed them in. Our job is to help God collect these shards and "fix the world." This concept introduced the idea that human actions can manifest change in the world. We have the power and ability to effect change when we choose to get involved. The Lurianic movement utilized the idea of *tikkun olam* to empower those who did not have access to higher levels of Jewish institutions (Yeshivot). Today, these ideas of *tikkun olam* can be utilized in the same ways. Your volunteer work is your physical manifestation of your acts of social responsibility within the world. You are doing your part to repair the world.

♥ *Volunteer to serve on a committee or the board for an organization that needs you.*

Send Out Pledge Cards for a Nonprofit

FOR THE PAST several years, I've volunteered for the American Heart Association neighborhood campaign each February. Responsibilities during the campaign entail sending out the cards provided by the organization to the neighbors. Donations come back to the volunteer, who is responsible for returning everything to the association by the established deadline.

• • • •

HELPING AN ORGANIZATION you care about send out their pledge cards is a great opportunity for anyone who doesn't like soliciting but still wants to help raise money. You don't directly solicit anyone; however, the letter comes from you, so your neighbors know you care about the charity you're representing. Organizations use this technique because they know people are more likely to give to those they know. By volunteering to do this kind of work, you educate your neighbors and help support a nonprofit.

♥ *Volunteer to help on a special project or event.*

Volunteering for Loaves and Fishes Centers' Valentine-A-Gram Program

THIS MITZVAH COINCIDED with my fifteenth wedding anniversary. My mother and I volunteered to deliver Valentine-A-Grams as part of a fundraiser for Loaves and Fishes, an organization that provides meals for homebound seniors. I've made a tradition of doing this every year, and I usually volunteer with my mom or my kids. One year my daughter invited a friend to come along, too. On the morning of the event, my mom called to say she wasn't feeling well and would not be able to join me. I was disappointed and feeling sorry for myself to have to volunteer alone. I got in the car, then turned on the radio and decided to make the most of the experience. The sun was shining, and I was able to quickly get into the spirit of the day, especially after my first few Valentine deliveries.

• • • •

DOING A VOLUNTEER job that requires time and effort can be enjoyable, especially when you do it with a friend or family member. The Valentine-A-Gram program always makes me happy, too, since I'm delivering a sweet message on a day when people are expressing their love for others. This year was eye-opening for me. I realized that I had made a commitment, and despite the fact that my volunteer partner had canceled, I still needed to show up. Once I changed my attitude, stopped feeling sorry for myself, and decided to enjoy myself, I did. When we work to consciously understand how we're feeling, we can help shift our thoughts at any moment.

♥ *Invite a friend to volunteer with you.*

VOLUNTEER WITH A VENGEANCE

Volunteering at a Garden Party

EVERY YEAR, OUR school hosts a "garden party." It's not really a party, but rather a chance to help weed the garden beds near my kids' school's first-grade classroom. It was very cold and rainy the morning of the party, so I was hoping the event might get canceled. By afternoon, the weather had cleared somewhat, and I knew we had to get the work done one way or another. I arrived at school with some extra layers for the kids and picked them up from their classrooms, ready to fulfill our commitment. Unlike me, they were perfectly happy being outside on a damp and overcast day.

Unfortunately, very few other parents came to help, so a handful of us worked to get the job done. The teachers were thrilled to have our assistance, and my son was even honored in school the next day for his help—an acknowledgment that made him very proud.

• • • •

FOR ME, THIS mitzvah wasn't altogether different from the Valentine-A-Gram program, except for the fact that it involved my children. Keeping my commitment to the teachers showed my children that I would follow through regardless of the weather. My son was the beneficiary of that experience. He loved the gratitude the teacher showed him when she thanked him for his help. Our kids hear what we say, but they learn from what we do. Making sure those things align is one of the more valuable ways we can show our kids by example.

♥ *Volunteer with your kids, your grandkids, niece, nephew, or a neighbor's child. Volunteering with children changes your perspective.*

Volunteering in an Elementary
School Classroom

AS PART OF their final project for their Revolutionary War history unit, my daughter and her classmates made a short documentary film called *How Colonial Girls Live*. When my daughter's teacher asked me to help with the videotaping, I was glad to be able to participate. Since I'm not especially tech-savvy, I was nervous how I'd do with the camera. The girls were in full colonial costume. We shot several scenes, including one outside in the schoolyard in a makeshift garden. My daughter and I enjoyed several funny moments that day. Later that year, her movie was nominated for a local award. I was gratified knowing I had helped.

• • • •

SPENDING TIME IN a child's classroom is always surprising. There is no better insight into what's happening at school than hanging around and volunteering. It's given me a greater awareness of the other children, and it helps me appreciate what the teachers do every day. There are lots of challenges to running a classroom. As budgets tighten, parent volunteers are even more essential. Our schools need our help immensely. Parents provide important support that teachers wouldn't otherwise get. Ask your teacher how you can help—even an hour can make a difference!

♥ *Volunteer your time in a classroom.*

MITZVAH 986

Volunteering to Speak on
Behalf of Your Organization

AT A PTO meeting in the spring, we got news that our district school budgets were going to be drastically cut. Our principal encouraged us to attend a listening session and voice our concerns. I volunteered to speak on behalf of our elementary school at that local school board budget committee meeting the following week.

• • • •

AS IT TURNS out, public speaking wasn't the hardest part of this mitzvah. Harder still was finding a unified statement that everyone agreed on. After several drafts and many intense conversations, we came up with our comments. The night of the meeting, other parents and I sat together and waited for our chance to speak. My heart was beating fast, as I convinced myself that I was going to get up there and be a confident spokesperson. Afterward, I was glad I had volunteered since it taught me several lessons about teamwork and unity. Sometimes taking on a volunteer role makes you step out of your comfort zone and grow in ways you don't expect. Leadership roles can be terrifying, but they also help you learn and expand your viewpoint. Even if taking on a leadership opportunity seems daunting, do it anyway!

♥ *Offer to speak on behalf of a volunteer organization.*

CHAPTER 4

····

CLEAR THE
CLUTTER

····

*"Giving a thousand gold coins to one
person and none to another does not
allow the giver the full opportunity to
acquire the quality of generosity—not
as full an opportunity as one who gives
a thousand gold coins on a thousand
different occasions . . . the repetition of
the acts a thousand times secures for that
individual the personal characteristic of
generosity."*

—MAIMONIDES
(COMMENTARY TO MISHNA,
AVOT 3:15)

· donations ·

WHEN IT COMES to donating, it's important to think beyond money. There are places that collect eyeglasses, computers, cars, furniture, used business clothing, shoes, cell phones, and so much more. In Portland, we have an organization called SCRAP (the School and Community Reuse Action Project), whose mission is to keep usable items out of the landfill. This is an organization I both donate to and buy from. My kids and I have gone there to buy art supplies for school projects, and we've also spent vacation days in their workshop making cool art projects out of reusable materials.

Donating your own used items actually serves a twofold purpose. Not only does it help you clear your mind and purge unnecessary clutter from your house, it also gives the used items a second life and puts them into the hands of someone else who will actually make use of the things you never think about anymore.

Most of us know that Goodwill or the Salvation Army can be great places to donate used items. However, it's worth the extra research to look for specialized organizations if you have specific items to donate. For example, Dress for Success is a great place that puts women's business clothes to good use. When I volunteered at Dress for Success, most of the volunteers drooled with envy at the gorgeous clothes that were donated. Make sure the clothes are current, and you can feel great knowing you will help a woman in need look and feel fantastic for her next job interview.

Sports equipment is another great thing to donate, and there are many organizations, including the Boys and Girls Club, that need all the equipment they can get their hands on. Another organization in California, Sports Gift, makes sure the sports equipment you donate is distributed to children in the United States and abroad.

If you have a pair of used eyeglasses, donate them to the Lions Club eyeglass recycling program, where they will be refurbished and passed along to clients in need.

Soles4Souls is a nonprofit with one simple mission: to collect shoes and give them away. Since its inception in 2005, this charity has given away over 5.5 million pairs of new and gently worn shoes. The shoes have been distributed to people in over 125 countries. Take a quick look in your closet and see if you have anything in there you haven't worn in years, or that no longer fits. Soles4Souls takes everything from pumps and flip-flops to boots and athletic shoes.

Environmentalists have rediscovered an old idea that was popular in the 1960s called "Giveaway Shops" or "Free Shops." These are physical shops where everything is free. These shops promote reuse and raise public awareness about consumer consumption. They are similar to secondhand stores that accept books, furniture, and other usable household items, but the merchandise in these shops is free, donated by others. They are typically run by volunteers, and they not only create an opportunity for recycling usable items, but they're also a great alternative to buying new. These types of stores have long been popular in Europe, and two of the most successful shops in the United States are the Freechange Store in Detroit, Michigan, and the Free Store in Baltimore, Maryland. The Free Store has been running for several years in temporary locations and continues to look for a permanent location.

WHEN I WAS a preteen, my father used to take my brother and me with him to the dump. I remember there was a small place where you could leave items for others to take. Sometimes we would see items we wanted, and other times we left items we didn't want for others. These dump shops still exist in many communities, and they're another option for getting rid of usable stuff if you can't find an alternative location to donate your still-usable goods.

Although we don't have any Free Shops currently running in Portland, we do have a well-known online nonprofit called Free Cycle, whose mission it is to connect people who are giving away items for free to others who might need them. We also have several tool libraries, which are popular in many major cities. These nonprofits provide tools to people in the community to "check out" and borrow for home projects. Though the tools that make these libraries work probably aren't 100 percent donated by the public, it's an example of a place that would certainly take your used tools. I'm simply suggesting that you think outside the box when you need to get rid of something that still works.

A few years ago, a friend of mine took this idea of connecting donors with end users to another level. She began a nonprofit called DonorsResource.org to connect people who have items to donate with nonprofits that can use those items. It's an online service that makes that valuable connection between people who have stuff to give away and companies or individuals in need. It's free to donors—and a brilliant idea! I used the service recently when we replaced our old dryer. Within two days we found a new home for our dryer, and we were happy to know that a transitional household would be putting it to good use. It's a win-win when you're getting rid of something, since you are generally trying to figure out how to get it out of your house, and someone else can really use and appreciate the items you don't want anymore. DonorsResource.org is expected to expand nationwide within a couple of years, so other cities will have the same opportunities as Portland. It's such a fabulous way to donate goods to those who can still use them.

Look around your house and see what you might have to donate. Make it into a game and find as many items as possible to give away. There are so many great options for donations that help others in need. So go ahead, start donating today!

Giving a Book to A Friend

A FRIEND OF mine was leaving for a trip and I thought she might enjoy a book for the vacation. I gifted her with my copy of a book I had recently read and loved.

· · · ·

THROUGHOUT THE COURSE of the mitzvah project, people often asked me what my first mitzvah was. They wanted to know if I had initially set out to do big mitzvahs and then realized it would be too hard and therefore started to tone it down. The truth is that from the outset I knew that my mitzvahs would be *small* acts of kindness. That was my intention from the beginning. The idea of tracking them gave me a chance to write and find solace and comfort after grief.

Indeed, giving, or even regifting, is a small gesture. But it's certainly a donation, and it's something that can help you share ideas and resources with people you know and love. Alternately, you can consider donating your used books to libraries, which can always make use of good books to build their collections. Giving away a copy of a book you've read, or a CD that you've enjoyed, can mean opening you up to a conversation you might not have otherwise had with a friend or loved one. This was, in fact, my first mitzvah, and my friend was touched by my small gesture.

♥ *Gift a book to a friend.*

CLEAR THE CLUTTER

Returning Bottles to Support the Local Elementary School

OUR LOCAL SUPERMARKET, Lamb's Thriftway, has a great program that earmarks donations from cans and bottles to several local schools. I did a large bottle return and was able to designate my daughter's elementary school as the recipient of the money. When I told my husband about it, he teased me that he should get credit for at least part of the mitzvah since he drank all the beer in the bottles I'd recycled.

• • • •

EVEN SOMETHING AS simple as bottles and cans can be turned into a mitzvah donation when there is a proper channel for doing so. This bottle collection program began several years ago when the schools in the Portland area were struggling under budget cuts. It brings in several thousand dollars each year. In addition, this same supermarket chain collects customers' Saturday shopping receipts and then they donate 2 percent of the total to the schools. It's a great way for community members to easily donate to a deserving local school. It's a win-win all around. Shoppers can feel good about returning their bottles or giving their shopping receipts, and the supermarket can partner with its customers to help with something we all care about—our kids' education.

♥ *Recycle your bottles. If your community doesn't currently have a system set up to donate the money to local schools, suggest it or donate the money directly to the school.*

Donating Requested Items to the School

THE PHYSICAL EDUCATION teacher at my children's school made a plea in the school newsletter for used bike helmets for the school's unicyclists in training. We had a few in our garage, so I packed them up and took them to the school. The Phys Ed teacher was beyond grateful, as it turned out that I was the only parent who heeded her important request.

• • • •

RECYCLING ITEMS YOU no longer need or use can be very beneficial to another person or organization. It's true that it can sometimes be hard to part with our stuff. How many things do you have stored away in your garage, attic, or storage unit saved for someday "just in case." Why is it so hard to purge our things? For a couple of reasons: First, we mistakenly feel that our stuff makes us more secure; in reality, it causes us to feel more weighted down. Second, we have an emotional attachment to our things, oftentimes especially our kids' things that serve to remind us of memories and times we'll never be able to recapture. Finally, the thought of purging can also be absolutely overwhelming. If you are ready to start purging and donating your usable items, grab a friend who has less emotional ties to your stuff than you do, or hire a professional organizer. Ask yourself this simple question: Do I currently use this item? If the answer is no, consider giving it away.

In the months after my father died, I was drawn to nesting. The nesting instinct is the urge to clean, tidy, and organize that usually occurs during pregnancy. However, experiencing the desire to nest after a loss is also common, since nesting is thought to be caused by both biological and emotional factors. It was very therapeutic to clean closets and organize my home during this time. Recycling and donating items in the process was very gratifying.

♥ *Donate to an organization with a specific request if you can meet the need.*

Encouraging My Son to Use His Own Money
to Purchase a Gift for a Child in Need

MY SON WAS eager to spend some of his recently received Hanukkah money, so I asked him how he would feel about using some of it to buy a toy for a needy child. His school had a toy drive for kids in need, so he agreed this would be a good way to spend some of his Hanukkah money and he picked the gift out himself. He and my daughter were both excited to wrap the gift and determine the age of the recipient. My son happily carried his present into school the following day.

• • • •

OVERINDULGED. THERE IS no other way to put it. My children and most other middle-class children fall into this category. They have toys, gadgets, and "stuff" coming out of their ears. My son has toys he never plays with and yet he can't part with them. At nine years old, his connection to his "stuff" is already unshakable. We haven't purchased a handheld video game for our son, but an older cousin passed down a GameBoy, so now he has one. Even trying hard to quell the tide, we still feel overrun by armloads of arts and craft supplies, LEGOs, Playmobil, and other assorted toys.

One of the lessons I'm working to teach my son and daughter is that "stuff" won't make them happy in the long run, and that there is a difference between wants and needs. My husband and I try to do this in our own lives through example, engaging in giving when we find opportunities that are appropriate. I know some parents who encourage the "one thing in, one thing out" rule. When your child gets a new toy, ask them to find one that they can give away. Teaching about giving and getting is hard work in our affluent society. I hope to instill these

CLEAR THE CLUTTER

lessons of giving to my children and help them realize not everyone, even within our own community, lives with such abundance.

♥ *Encourage your children to give some of their birthday or holiday gift money to a charity or to use some of it to buy items to donate.*

Donating to a Charity in Honor of a Friend
Who Received a Donated Kidney

THIS WASN'T MY mitzvah, but I include it here to show how deep a mitzvah can run, and to show the ripple effect certain types of good deeds can have on others. In this case, an acquaintance in the Jewish community donated a healthy kidney to a friend of mine who was in need. I was so touched by this selfless donation that I decided to find a way to show my support by sending a donation in their honor—donor and recipient—to a Jewish charity.

• • • •

WHEN I FIRST learned that an acquaintance was planning to donate his kidney to a friend in need, I immediately thought about what I would do in the same situation. Would I donate my own organ to a friend? I honestly wasn't sure I would do the same. But I was so moved by this donation that I wanted to find a small way of honoring such a courageous and selfless action.

In Judaism, a donation of an organ to another is seen as one of the ultimate acts of kindness. There's a phrase from the Babylonian Talmud that reads, "Whoever saves a life, it is considered as if he saved an entire world" (Sanhedrin 4:8 [37a]).

It's precisely because life is held so sacred, though, that the subject of organ donation is complicated. There is an important distinction between donated organs from a living person versus from someone who has died. In Judaism, there is a concept called *Pikuach Nefesh*. This concept is derived from the biblical verse, "Neither shall you stand by the blood of your neighbor" (Leviticus 19:16). According to *Pikuach Nefesh*, a person is obligated to do everything in their power to save a life in jeopardy, even donate bodily organs. In most Jewish communities, a living person is thus permitted to donate organs they can live without, like a kidney. This is seen as admissible, even altruistic. Donating body parts that renew themselves, like blood or bone marrow, is also acceptable in most Jewish communities. It gets more complicated, however, when someone who has died has chosen to donate organs. It would seem that if saving a life is of the utmost importance, then donating organs after death would be obligatory. However, Jewish law states that an organ can only be taken from a person whose heart is no longer beating—*and* if it will immediately be used to save a life. If these two criteria of Jewish law are met, then it is acceptable for a deceased person to donate their organs. However, the medical reality is that organs don't always get used immediately to save a life. Sometimes they are used for other purposes, like medical research. Herein lies the controversy of this opportunity.

I personally struggle with the idea of giving blood, much less giving an organ. When giving blood during pregnancy, I always had to lie down so I didn't pass out. Needless to say, the idea of volunteering to give blood makes me very queasy. Nevertheless, hearing about this man who'd donated a kidney to a friend did give me pause. I wondered what I could do given my own personal squeamishness. As I contemplated this, I had to ask myself, is doing a mitzvah that is truly out of your comfort zone better than one that comes easily to you?

Later that week, when I discussed this with my then nine-year-old daughter, she said, "Mommy, there are like a thousand other mitzvahs you can do, so you don't *have* to do one that makes you uncomfortable." Such profound insight at such a young age!

THIS MITZVAH BROUGHT up many conversations about blood and organ donation around our community. Many people aren't able to be organ donors, or even blood donors. Yet, there is a tremendous need for both. While researching this chapter, I learned about HOD (*Halachic* Organ Donor Society), a nonprofit organization whose mission is to save lives by increasing organ donations from Jews to the general population. Also, Chaya Lipschutz started kidneymitzvah.com after donating her own kidney to a stranger. She continues to help others in need of kidneys. Get educated about this subject, talk to your clergyperson, and sign up to donate blood or become an organ donor, if that's something you feel comfortable doing.

♥ *Learn about organ and blood donation options. Sign up to give.*

Organizing a Mitten Tree Project for the
Clients of Dress for Success, Oregon

IN OCTOBER, I had an idea to participate in some Christmas giving. I shared it with my daughter, who loves the Christmas holiday and finds it difficult that we don't have a tree, stockings, or Christmas decorations like other kids. I decided it would be fun to create a mitten tree for the clients of the Dress for Success program I volunteer for. We'd find out what clients needed or wanted for Christmas, and then we'd work with my networking group of approximately fifty women to try to gather the money and gifts. I hoped my daughter would help me make the one-dimensional paper tree with paper mittens on a bulletin board that I could carry to my meeting for the women to choose from.

I gathered the art supplies for our project. Immediately, my daughter began to complain. "I didn't volunteer for this, how soon will we be done?" she whined. We continued working despite her complaints. I distracted her by reading some of the requested items, which included dance pants for a thirteen-year-old girl. "How does someone who needs our gifts pay for dance lessons for their child?" she asked. "Maybe a scholarship," I told her. Another woman wanted a Burger King gift certificate so she and her husband could go out to dinner. My daughter commented that she didn't think Burger King was a very special place to go out to dinner. Another woman requested a gift card for gas. My daughter continued cutting mittens and a few minutes later said, "Wow, Mommy, I am really lucky. We have a house, we have food to eat, we aren't worried about paying our bills or buying gas. I am glad we are doing this together." Then she chose a mitten for a grandmother raising her grandson who'd requested a winter snowsuit for the boy.

In December, a thank-you note arrived from the volunteer coordinator at Dress for Success. She told me that seventy-two women had received gifts through the mitten project. To this day, this is one of my favorite and most memorable mitzvahs.

• • • •

BEING A CATALYST to make something happen is incredibly rewarding. It requires seeing an opportunity and taking initiative. This mitzvah was gratifying on two levels: first, knowing that seventy-two women received a special gift for the holidays, and second, that my actions taught my daughter a valuable lesson. My role in this mitzvah was being the person who got the ball rolling. The coordination meant collecting and gathering the goods, but this was relatively easy and didn't even take that much time. The outcome from these simple actions was huge. The recipients and donors alike felt blessed by the opportunity, and I had the pleasure of knowing I'd been the catalyst and a teacher.

♥ *Create a mitten tree project at your school or organization.*

Donating Supplies

EACH DECEMBER, THE second-grade teachers send home a request for supplies for the annual gingerbread house–making project. They ask for graham crackers, fluff, marshmallows, and other assorted sugary supplies. I dropped off two boxes of graham crackers for the project and volunteered for clean-up duty.

• • • •

I AM A stickler when it comes to sweets. I have tried diligently to teach my kids about proper nutrition and eating healthy foods, which doesn't always make me a popular mom. For years, I have donated my time and supplies to events like the second-grade barbecue, which is all about chips, fruit snacks, cookies, and hot dogs, and has, of course, very little emphasis on nutrition. The gingerbread house project is a complete sugarfest. For me, donating and volunteering at these activities has meant supporting school-sanctioned events I don't completely believe in, but the reality is that these events will go on with or without our help, so why not volunteer—and participate in school activities your kids are involved in.

I have shared my thoughts on this subject with my children, in part because I want them to understand how giving our time and support is important, even when we're not 100 percent on board for a given project. I am certain that both of my kids have internalized my views on the subject. Sometimes we give even when it's not easy.

♥ *Donate whenever asked. If you don't support the cause and decide to still donate, discuss it with your family.*

CHAPTER 5

DOLLARS AND SENSE

"No act of kindness, no matter how small, is ever wasted."

—AESOP, FROM THE FABLE
THE LION AND THE MOUSE

· *money* ·

O VER THE COURSE of the mitzvah project, there were many mitzvahs that were obvious, like helping poor, sick, or elderly people. Giving money to *tzedakah* was another given. In Judaism, we use the word *tzedakah* when we refer to giving money to charity. The word *tzedakah* literally translates to "righteousness" or "justice," and a *tzaddik* is a person who fulfills their moral and religious obligation whether they want to or not. In common practice, however, it's about giving to a poor or needy person, or other worthwhile causes. The idea of justice behind this giving, however, connotes that all our wealth comes from a higher place, and we may not understand the basis of it. The fact that some of us have more and others have less doesn't have any bearing on who is more deserving.

In March 2007, three months into the mitzvah project, I decided to review my initial one hundred mitzvahs to see how many were money-related. I was also interested to see how many mitzvahs required only my time and how many took less than five minutes. This initial review gave rise to self-reflection about the nature of giving money and whether giving more or less made a mitzvah more or less valuable. For instance, I often put spare change in the collection boxes at the super-market or drugstore, and initially I wasn't sure whether giving a few quarters now and then really counted. In contemplating these actions, however, I decided that regardless of the amount you give, even a few quarters is still giving. I recently found out that a Portland based Meals On Wheels charity with more than thirty-five collection sites through-out the Portland metro area collects over $20,000 annually in their coin canisters. It's enough to feed their entire clientele of five thousand seniors for one day. Not bad for nickels, dimes, and quarters.

Out of my first one hundred mitzvahs, approximately one-fourth of them involved money. Three-fourths were just my time, and of those, almost twenty took less than five minutes. What this revealed to me is that mitzvah-making can be a quick and easy endeavor, something that will hopefully inspire everyone to want to participate in more daily acts of kindness.

Money will always be a powerful tool in doing mitzvahs. Every organization needs money to do their important work. While I noticed that money wasn't the only important tool when it came to doing mitzvahs, it certainly does have its place where acts of kindness are concerned. So why not work to give a little more money when possible? Find ways you can donate money instead of spending money on gifts you might give to people, like flowers, chocolates, or other kinds of items. Sometimes people are worried that if they don't give a gift to someone, and instead donate to a charity in their honor, the would-be recipient might be offended. If more people spent gift money on donations, however, it would change that perception. If you do your homework and find meaningful organizations that your family member or friend cares about, you might find they are truly touched.

It has become common practice for bar and bat mitzvah children to choose organizations that they care about and ask others to donate in their honor. It creates a meaningful connection for the child at this important time in their lives. I read a wonderful article about a bar mitzvah boy who had lost several grandparents to cancer, including a grandfather he was especially close to. Prior to his bar mitzvah, he had asked his mom to arrange a tour of a local cancer center. There he learned about a new drug that was being researched to provide a better course of treatment for cancer patients. In his bar mitzvah speech, he shared with 350 guests his personal history of how cancer had affected his family. He explained the drug and its implications. He compared his grandparents' enslavement of fighting cancer to the Torah portion he was reading that week. He found a connection in a thousand-year old text to something personal in his own life. Guests from his bar mitzvah sent more than 140 gifts to the cancer center he had designated in honor of his bar mitzvah. Within a few days of the bar mitzvah, the cancer center had already received over $25,000. This story shows the power of asking and the power of giving.

After the earthquake in Haiti in January 2010, we saw a form of giving catapult to a new level. That is mobile giving. Why was it so effective? Because it was effortless. People heard the request to text their $10 donations via cell phone on Twitter, Facebook, and news broadcasts. Immediately, they pulled out their phones and, presto, they made their donations. Because there was a simple opportunity for people to give, they did so quickly and felt that they had made a difference. Within days of the earthquake, the American Red Cross alone had received more than $4 million worth of donations through $10 texts. By February 2010, that number had increased to $32 million donated to the American Red Cross, thanks to public service announcements showed on television and a promotion during the Super Bowl. And that was only the American Red Cross; many other agencies also received money for Haiti relief through texts.

If you think your $10 doesn't matter, you are wrong. Each of those $10 donations raised an unprecedented amount of money for many different organizations. Every gift matters. Technology is changing the way people give their money, and it will be interesting to see how this changes the future of fundraising. In Judaism, giving money is not only a generous act, but also an act of justice. It is our duty and obligation to give *tzedakah*.

Giving *Tzedakah* at Synagogue

ONE MONTH AFTER my father died, I did something impulsive. I had been attending morning services at our synagogue on a regular basis so I could recite the *Kaddish* for my father. It is customary to leave some money for *tzedakah* at the end of services. I usually gave whatever was in my wallet, some coins or a dollar. This particular day, I was feeling very grateful. I had gotten a full and restful night's sleep and had received an honor that morning at services. When I looked in my wallet, I saw that I didn't have any change or small bills—only a $20. I decided that rather than leave nothing, I would leave the $20. It felt astonishing. I was even giddy when I walked out of synagogue. I knew according to Maimonides' Eight Levels of Giving, which I mentioned previously in Chapter 1, I had given at one of the highest levels possible, anonymously.

• • • •

YOU MIGHT ALREADY throw a few coins into charity cans. You might realize, like me, it's an easy opportunity to give. But actually, taking out a twenty-dollar bill—enough money to buy two lunches, a night of baby-sitting, or a piece of clothing—was different. I knew I was giving "something" more tangible with that donation. I delighted in thinking about the person who would open the can, since I knew that people mostly give a few coins, or dollar bills at the most. If five, ten, or a hundred dollars is a stretch, try that. I can assure you it feels very different from putting small change in the can. I honestly felt like I had won the lottery that morning—and the feeling lasted all day long.

♥ *Give away more money today than you usually do. It doesn't matter if it's one, five, ten, or one hundred dollars.*

Donating Money in Honor
of a Friend's Marriage

WE HAD THE interesting opportunity to attend a friend's second wedding to the same man—a Jewish celebration after the man converted to Judaism. They'd had a secular ceremony several years earlier, so this celebration was all about a community celebration and the Jewish traditions. It was a festive day, and we were thrilled to be able to share this occasion with them. Since this was a second wedding, we opted to donate in their honor to an organization we knew was important to them.

• • • •

THERE ARE MANY occasions for giving gifts and making donations in honor or memory of someone. One of my mitzvah mentors, Jewish educator Danny Siegel (www.dannysiegel.com), has come up with a wonderful list of ideas that detail times when you might give *tzedakah* rather than a traditional gift.

Occasions for Giving *Tzedakah*
by Danny Siegel

A. Concerning other people

1. In honor of a birth, baby naming, bar mitzvah, bat mitzvah, confirmation, wedding, anniversary, or other joyous occasion

2. In honor of a patriarch or matriarch who has reached a significant birthday: sixtieth, seventieth, seventy-fifth, eightieth, ninetieth, or one hundreth up to one hundred twentieth

3. To extend wishes for the recovery of someone who is sick

4. In memory of someone who has passed away

5. In honor of major events in a person's life: graduation, new job, etc.

B. Occasions in your own life

1. Bar mitzvah, bat mitzvah, confirmation, wedding, anniversary, or other joyous occasion

2. Reaching a significant birthday

3. Upon recovery from an illness

4. In honor of your own graduation, new job, etc.

5. Before candle lighting on Friday night

6. Before Jewish or non-Jewish holidays, specifically to people and agencies that provide food for the poor on those holidays

7. At synagogue or church when you attend services

8. Upon arriving safely from a trip

9. Upon receiving a foundation grant or inheriting a sum of money or receiving any money as a gift

♥ *Send a donation in honor of a special occasion with a gift to a meaningful organization.*

Donating More to a Homeless Vendor Selling Newspapers

IN PORTLAND, WE have an organization called Street Roots. It is a local publication written, distributed, and sold by homeless people. Many of the vendors sit outside of our local supermarkets and sell the papers to the public. I learned from a vendor that they keep seventy cents for every one-dollar paper they sell. When I found out that they also get to keep anything above and beyond the dollar, I made it a practice to give the vendor an extra dollar.

• • • •

THE STREET ROOTS vendors are working to make a living so they may get or keep themselves off the street. Giving a little extra money, which they can keep, just supports their efforts. After celebrating our anniversary with a hotel stay downtown, my husband and I ran into a Street Roots vendor outside of a local bookstore. When I paid for the paper, he mentioned there was an article about him in the edition he was selling. The article talked about how he lived in the woods and how a candle is the one item that helps him keep away the loneliness he feels in the darkness at night. I decided we needed to buy him some candles, and I was thrilled to find out that the bookstore carried them. When we brought them out to him, he was visibly touched. He told us we had no idea how much he appreciated the gift. Purchasing that newspaper and reading the article allowed me to learn and help this gentleman in a way that I otherwise never could have.

♥ *Donate to a homeless shelter or organization that helps men and women get off the streets.*

Creating Charity Boxes for *Tzedakah* Collecting

DURING THE SUMMER, as an arts and crafts project, my kids created *tzedakah* boxes out of old tea cans for each of their favorite charities, which included their summer camp, a puppet theater, and the Oregon Humane Society. Each Friday night, they gathered spare change from around the house and chose which charity they would like to put money toward. They chose their summer camp many Fridays since they love the camp so much. Last year, I told them I would match any money they saved during the year to give back to the camp at the annual auction. When my daughter counted the money they'd saved at the end of one year she was thrilled to see that they had saved $39. She was over-the-moon excited when she realized her "matched" gift would equal almost $80.

• • • •

THIS MITZVAH TURNED out to be a fantastic opportunity to teach our children about money, saving, and giving. The previous year our family had donated $75 to the kids' camp during the annual auction. This year, since the kids had saved half that amount through their weekly *tzedakah* savings, we were able to donate more. They felt empowered by how much money they had saved and realized that a small amount saved each week can add up to a large number.

♥ *Make tzedakah/charity cans with your kids. Pick a day and time each week that you will put some change in. We do it on Friday nights. You could also do it on the day your children get their allowance. Match what they save to give to a charity your family chooses.*

Telling a Waiter about a Bill Discrepancy

WHEN WE EAT out at a restaurant, I always double-check the bill before we pay to be sure that it is correct. Most of the time the bill is correct, but during the mitzvah project I had a couple of occasions when I discovered discrepancies with a bill. In both cases, our waiters were very grateful when I brought it to their attention. In one case, the bill was correct, but in the other case we had been charged too little.

• • • •

"DO NOT STEAL" is a biblical imperative. It is also a mitzvah. Cheating someone is another form of stealing. After seeing the bill and realizing there was a discrepancy, it would have been easy to pay the incorrect amount and leave. But I chose to tell the waiter instead. It reminded me of another time at Target several years ago. I'd been looking at purses and slung the one I liked over my shoulder right alongside the purse I'd come in with. I didn't notice and walked out without paying for it. When I got to the car and was unpacking my bags, I realized the Target purse was still slung over my shoulder. Talk about a distracted young mother. The purse was hot pink and quite cute. I was late and couldn't go immediately back into the store, but I did go back the next day. Even though I had succeeded in "stealing" this purse, I knew there was no way I could use my hot pink purse—that others would surely notice and comment on—without going back and paying for it. Even without a visible item like a hot pink purse to remind you of your offense, however unintentional, paying the correct amount on a restaurant bill, or any bill for that matter, is the honest and right thing to do.

♥ *Look at your shopping bills and restaurant tabs and report any discrepancies.*

Giving Money to a Friend Leaving for Israel

A FRIEND OF mine was leaving for Israel to celebrate a family wedding, and I gave her a few dollars. It's not the amount that matters so much as the custom that's behind it. I learned about this Jewish custom when I was in college. My boyfriend at the time gave me a few dollars when I was leaving for a trip to ensure my safe travels. The idea is that when you arrive safely at your destination, you will donate that money locally.

It seems I only remember this custom when a friend goes to Israel, but I like the idea for anytime someone is traveling.

• • • •

JUDAISM TEACHES THAT one who is giving *tzedakah* is immune from harm. Rabbi Elazar ben Azariah, a 10th century rabbinic sage said, "No harm happens to people on Mitzvah missions, neither en route to the Mitzvah, nor on the way back" (Pesachim 8b). This idea has led to a belief that if someone is about to embark on a trip and is taking *tzedakah*, they will be protected on their journey. Even if it's more tradition than anything, I love this concept. An individual embarking on a trip with a mission to deliver *tzedakah* on the other end is somehow protected. The next time you hear someone is traveling, give them a dollar or two to arrive safely at their destination.

♥ *Give money to family, friends, or a colleague leaving on a trip. Ask them to give the money to a local nonprofit when they arrive at their destination.*

DOLLARS AND SENSE

Donating to the Leukemia and Lymphoma Society

MY SON CAME home from school particularly excited because his school was raising money for the Leukemia and Lymphoma Society with a fundraiser called Pennies for Patients. He gathered all his money and then began searching for more pennies around the house. He also decided he wanted to use some of the *tzedakah* money that he'd collected each Friday night for this cause. I was so proud to witness his determination and excitement about this fundraiser, and it was contagious, too, because he was able to get his sister into the spirit and the two of them eagerly scoured the house looking for any change they could donate to the cause.

• • • •

THIS COLLECTION GOT started by a friend of ours whose daughter had cancer as an infant. Each year they have organized a drive at our school for the Leukemia and Lymphoma Society. When we organize or participate in these *tzedakah* activities, we are teaching our children how important giving is. This was one of those times during the mitzvah project when I just sat back and smiled that my kids were taking their own initiative for giving. My son's excitement over this project stood in stark contrast to the time he was asked to bring canned food to school. That time he felt obligated to give. This mitzvah, on the other hand, hit a nerve with him and he was eager to collect as much change as he could—and his enthusiasm and excitement was contagious. Giving begets giving.

♥ *Donate to a new charity that's important to a friend or colleague.*

Donating Money in Honor of a Special Occasion

MY HUSBAND AND I often celebrate our anniversary by going out to dinner, and if we can, taking a night or two away from the children to reconnect. We aren't much into the personal gift giving since we'd rather spend the time together celebrating. During the mitzvah project, my husband gave me a special and unexpected gift. He donated money in honor of our anniversary to an international children's charity. All the talk about mitzvahs over the past year had brought the idea of giving in honor of a special event to the forefront of his mind, and he thought it would make me happy. It was a wonderful treat to receive the note in the mail acknowledging the donation.

• • • •

IN SEVENTEEN YEARS of marriage, I have *always* been the one who makes the donations to charities. I answer or make the calls, write the checks, and take care of any of the tasks related to our monetary or physical family donating. Of course, it is our combined family money, and we often discuss how we would like to give, but it seems as if I am the one who makes the effort to actually do the donating. Imagine my delight, then, when my husband took the initiative to donate in honor of our anniversary. He had learned about the charity on a radio broadcast, had done some research, and knew that I would prefer that to a present. The gift actually brought me to tears. I was thrilled about making an impact in this way, but also from knowing that the small actions we do influence those around us. Realizing that I was influencing my husband in this way warmed my heart.

♥ *For your next birthday or anniversary, ask that others give to a charity on your behalf.*

DOLLARS AND SENSE

Returning Dropped Change to an Elder

AT THE GROCERY store, an older lady dropped a few coins. I knelt down to help her pick up her money. She didn't speak English very well, but she was obviously grateful to me, as she smiled and bowed and gestured her appreciation.

• • • •

OFTEN THE LITTLE things we do to help someone else have a greater effect than we might imagine. This act was barely even a blip in my life. In fact, if I hadn't been recording mitzvahs for my blog, it probably wouldn't have been something I'd even noticed or give thought to. Yet this woman was so grateful for my help, as her aging body would have struggled to kneel down to the ground to retrieve her money. These types of opportunities are everywhere. They are just small incidents in our lives and yet they are truly the activities that connect us to one another, both strangers and friends.

♥ *Pick up change or anything else that you can, and bring ease to an elder.*

CHAPTER 6

.....

SLOW DOWN

"Have you ever noticed that anybody driving slower than you is an idiot and anyone driving faster than you is a maniac?"

—GEORGE CARLIN

· *driving* ·

THE RULES OF the road vary significantly depending on where you live. Out in the country, where I grew up, kids as young as ten or eleven operate power equipment—tractors, snowmobiles, or old trucks. By the time I got my license on the day I turned sixteen, I'd already driven a snowmobile through the back pasture and the rural areas around our house. My father taught me everything I needed to know about driving in our manual transmission 1975 Dodge Plymouth. We practiced shifting, three-point turns, parallel parking, and 360s in the high school parking lot on a layer of freshly plowed snow.

Getting my license meant taking on more responsibilities, since now there was another driver in the house to help ensure that my brother and I both got wherever we needed to go. My dad also had a yellow VW Bug in the 1980s, complete with running boards. Dad used to take us out on "adventure rides," which involved standing outside of the car on the running boards as my father grabbed us by the waist through the rolled-down driver's seat window, while manning the steering wheel down our one-mile dirt road. It was exhilarating, and I can still remember the way the wind caught my hair and the absolute thrill of those special rides.

Driving played a vital role in our family growing up. My father was a good teacher, and I became a confident driver as a result. He taught me to parallel park, a skill I use daily and still thank him for. Some of those times we spent driving were, in fact, the best memories I have of our time spent together.

Whether you grew up in the city or the country, you no doubt remember who taught you to drive. And because we're a driving country, driving mitzvahs abound. Once you start paying attention, you'll notice that there are opportunities to practice them nearly every day.

They can happen when you choose to be a polite driver, when you use your vehicle to help another person out, or when you help a nonprofit provide their services or goods by using your car.

Drive Someone to a Doctor's Appointment

THIS MITZVAH OFTEN presents itself when you have to help out a friend or family member. This particular day I stumbled upon the chance to help out when I was visiting with my rabbi and his wife over breakfast. The rebbetzin typically offers me a meal, no matter what time of day I stop by. On this visit, while we were eating, she asked if I could drive her husband to the clinic to have some blood work done. The doctor's office was only a few blocks from their home, but the rabbi and rebbetzin were elderly and no longer driving. It was a simple request, and something I felt honored to do.

• • • •

THIS MITZVAH ENDED up being a gift, as it was an opportunity to spend some one-on-one time with my rabbi. Whether you're driving someone you know in a professional capacity or a friend or family member, helping a person do something they can't do themselves can be a real treat. Since we ended up having to wait for the rabbi's paperwork to be processed, I got a chance to spend over an hour talking with him. It isn't every day that you have a rabbi's undivided attention. We discussed an upcoming *D'var Torah* (brief Bible commentary) I was giving in honor of my father's birthday a few weeks later. I shared my ideas and he gave me helpful suggestions.

If someone asks, don't look at the request as an obligation, but as an opportunity to connect. And if you sense that someone might need a ride somewhere but they are too proud or shy to ask, offer and see what happens. Remember that there is such a thing as cultivating good karma—and you'll undoubtedly find yourself in a situation at some point when you need a ride. I certainly hope this is a mitzvah I'll receive on occasions when I can't drive!

♥ *Drive someone to an appointment, the grocery store, or on an errand they couldn't otherwise do without a ride.*

Let Another Driver In

THIS MITZVAH—ALLOWING another driver to cut in—is actually something I do rather often. Whether we're talking about letting someone merge or turn into traffic, too few people actually let others go in front of them! And yet it's so easy. It's also a gesture that makes people feel seen and accommodated and good about other drivers on the road. Too often we're so busy *not* letting people in that we end up with road rage or fatigue from coping with the intensity of being out on the road. When I first moved to Portland from Boston, I was pleasantly surprised at how patient and gracious drivers are here, but certainly that's not true all the time. I have to admit that this mitzvah is much easier when I'm not racing through my day. I can be just as inconsiderate as anyone when I am running late. When I notice my driving manners diminish, it's a good reminder to myself to slow down.

• • • •

TOWARD THE END of the mitzvah project, I was late driving to a meeting. I had already pulled over once for a passing fire truck when I recognized I was behind a funeral processional. At the next green traffic light, a police officer stopped my lane of traffic so the funeral processional could successfully pass through the light together. I watched in disbelief as the car ahead of me zipped through the processional to get onto the freeway ramp. I took a deep breath and realized that I felt badly for that person. The funeral procession gave me a chance to think about the fact that being late to my meeting was nothing in the grand scheme of things. I reflected on this group of people who had recently lost a loved one and my thoughts turned to my father, who learned to drive in New York City, and yet by the time he taught me to drive, he'd adopted the mentality of a country driver. He was an aggressive driver who was also polite and let people in, and for the most part he never screamed or cursed at the cars in front of him. After a few moments, I was able to get grounded and be on my way. Yes, I was late to the meeting, but I didn't feel harried or overworked. I simply apologized and it wasn't a big deal at all.

♥ *Signal to a driver today and let them go in front of you.*

Help Someone Who's Forgotten
Something at Home

I'D BEEN LOOKING forward to this day for a long time because we were finally getting some long overdue yard work done at our house. It was an unseasonably warm May day, and the landscaper had arrived early with two additional workers. It wasn't long, however, before he realized that he'd forgotten the keys to the lockbox on his trunk that held all his tools. I saw that he was struggling to figure out what to do and I asked him what was happening. He explained that he didn't want to take time out from the job to run home for the keys, but it would mean that some of the things he'd hoped to get to might have to wait for another time. I asked if I could drive him home to get his keys so that his guys could get started and he wouldn't feel like he was cutting too much into the day's work.

• • • •

MY HUSBAND AND I know our landscaper pretty well. He'd done amazing work for us every spring for years. He was so grateful for the offer of a ride, which, of course, was a win-win situation, and it was fun for me because it gave me an opportunity to have more than just a passing conversation with him. He told me about his family and children and about his gardening experience. It only took twenty minutes round-trip, and it provided the unexpected gift of deepening our working relationship.

♥ *Be the lift someone needs when they've left something behind.*

Carpool

EACH SUMMER MY kids attend a day camp that's a bit out of our way. To help defray the increasing cost of gas (and because it's good for the environment), I generally like to arrange a carpool. This July day it was my friend's day to pick up and she dropped in to say hello before making her way home. When she returned to her car, it wouldn't start, and her daughter was supposed to be at a class that was beginning just twenty minutes later. I offered to take her daughter to the class while she waited with the rest of the kids for her husband to come pick her up. Luckily, the problem turned out to be with her key, so when her husband showed up with the spare, they were able to be on their way as soon as I returned.

· · · ·

LEND A HAND. Offer to help someone in a pinch. We are presented with opportunities to give back every single day. We simply have to get good at recognizing those opportunities for what they are. Helping each other makes our days more fulfilling and colors our lives with the positive giving we all crave. A few weeks later, my car wouldn't start after camp pickup and another parent offered jumper cables to get me started. I thought about the truism that what goes around comes around. Lending a hand is part of life. Sometimes you give and sometimes you get.

♥ *Lend a hand when someone is in a pinch.*

MITZVAH 821

Give Someone Else's Kid a Ride Home

WE CELEBRATED MY son's eighth birthday party at a fun pizza place with a giant indoor play structure about a half-hour drive from our house. After the party, one of the kid's parents called to say that they were in a bind and couldn't come pick up their son right away. I offered to take him home, even though the boy's house was another hour round-trip. This was not a moment of feeling particularly warmhearted with the mitzvah at hand, but upon seeing his grateful parents, I realized how much it meant to them and how important it is that we create community by treating one another's kids as we would our own.

• • • •

HAVE YOU EVER offered to do something and then wished you hadn't? You might have even wondered, *How did I get myself into this situation?* After hosting a birthday party with eight kids at a noisy pizza place, the last thing I wanted to do was drive across town to drop off another child. In the end, however, it turned out differently than I'd expected.

In Judaism, we generally observe a person's death by the Hebrew date rather than the traditional date from the calendar year, so the anniversary of someone's death will change from year to year. Even so, the actual day my father died, December 1, 2006, coincided with my son's sixth birthday. I expected that my son's birthday would carry the weight of my father's death, even if I intended to formally observe the Hebrew date of his passing. Perhaps that's why in the end, the extra drive provided me the first chance that day to quietly catch my breath and give me space to reflect on my father. This mitzvah gave me something I hadn't consciously realized I needed that day.

♥ *Go the extra mile.*

Compliment Someone for
Their Outstanding Service

DURING WINTER BREAK, we rented a van from a local car rental agency. It was a special request because we needed something large enough to hold our family of four plus my in-laws. We'd been told that the van would be available around 1 PM, and we'd arranged our day accordingly. That morning, we received a call around 9 AM from the agency letting us know that the pickup time had been delayed. The employee promised she would be in frequent communication to keep us updated. She called us, as promised, at least three times, and we eventually got our van around 4 PM. When we picked it up, I made a point to tell the manager how much we had appreciated the employee keeping us updated on the status of the vehicle.

• • • •

WE ARE CONSTANTLY waiting for things. Whether it's a car repair, a doctor's appointment, our kid's activities, or a service of some other kind, we spend hours of our lives waiting. Receiving updates helps ease the discomfort of not knowing when the waiting will end. In this case, the employee's desire to make sure we were well-informed turned the annoyance of our car being delayed into a wonderful opportunity to enjoy our day. Because she kept us updated, we made plans around town. We took a morning swim and had lunch at one of my in-laws' favorite lunch spots. I hope her manager let her know how grateful we were since her customer service was exemplary and deserved special recognition.

♥ *Commend someone on a job well done—let them know that they're* *appreciated.*

Help an Acquaintance Perform
a Mitzvah for a Friend

ONE OF MY dear friends, an old college roommate, had surgery and had to spend some time recovering at home. Her mother flew into town to help out, and so did one of her childhood girlfriends. My friend asked me if I could pick up her childhood friend from the airport. It was a horrible rainy day, but the company of this new acquaintance made it all worthwhile. We chatted the entire way, and I learned some new things about our mutual friend! I shared my mitzvah project with her and applauded her for the mitzvah she was performing by coming to help a friend in need. She was quick to turn it back to me and say that my picking her up from the airport was an equally valuable mitzvah.

• • • •

HOW MUCH DO you appreciate a personal pickup from the airport? I know I appreciate it a lot, especially on the return trip home! One year, our family traveled to Florida to visit my in-laws. It was well after midnight when we arrived with two small children and luggage for an extended winter vacation. We were tired and crabby, and I was never so grateful to see a car waiting for us. My in-laws had arranged to send a driver, which was the most amazing gift we could have received in that moment. Picking someone up from the airport is an act of generosity, and it's important never to assume that the person who's picking you up isn't going out of their way. Make sure to express gratitude, and when you can do this for someone else, take the time to make it happen. We're all grateful for safety and ease when we're coming off a flight and a day of traveling.

♥ *Pick someone up at the airport.*

CHAPTER 7

···· ····

MY HOME
AWAY FROM
HOME

···· ····

A rabbi's young son sat on the floor of his father's office watching him write a sermon.

"How do you know what to say?" the boy asked.

"Why, God tells me," his father replied.

"Then why do you keep crossing things out?"

· synagogue-related mitzvahs ·

IN THE MONTHS after my father died, I had the opportunity to say the mourner's *kaddish,* or prayer, in his memory. I attended more than a few synagogues during those months. Partly this was due to my children's schedule, and partly it had to do with the fact that my synagogue at the time did not count women in their *minyan.* A *minyan* is a quorum of ten people necessary to fulfill certain religious obligations in Judaism. In non-egalitarian synagogues, only men are counted. Not being counted in the *minyan* was more than just a frustration to me. It felt restrictive and outdated, and it didn't occur to me how important it was to be counted in this way until I was saying *kaddish* myself. In some of the less traditional synagogues, I was welcomed by older members of the congregation during my time of grief. I felt a kinship with many of the older members who were there for their own personal reasons, some saying *kaddish* and some just participating in this daily community. About a year later, our family did join one of these synagogues, and it has been a comfortable place for all of us.

One morning at a service, I was standing near a woman with a ten-month-old baby. She had come to synagogue to say the mourner's prayer for her grandmother who had recently passed. Although it is only required that immediate members of the deceased (siblings, parents, children, or spouse) say the mourner's prayer, anyone may choose to say it. The short mourner's prayer is recited at various transition points throughout the service. During the final *Kaddish* prayer, the baby began to cry and needed to be picked up. The rabbi asked if he could lend a hand. He gently picked up the baby and cooed and spoke to the child, telling her that her mommy was praying. The baby watched him so intently that the woman was able to say the prayer with focused energy and presence. The whole scene brought tears to my eyes. When we do a mitzvah, not only do the giver and receiver benefit, but oftentimes onlookers do, as well.

. . . .

Offer Some Words of Wisdom

IN HONOR OF my father's birthday, what would have been his seventy-first, I gave a *D'var Torah*, or a brief commentary, on the week's Torah reading at a monthly women's service that met at the local Jewish Day School. It was an opportunity to volunteer and to share some thoughts on the text as it related to my own life. I compared the story of the Jewish people being asked to bring gifts to the Temple to the ways in which each of us is called to share our own gifts in the world. I shared how my father's dying process became an opportunity for him to share his gifts with those he loved. It hadn't occurred to me before that time that knowing death is near could turn into such a beautiful chance to connect and share. My father had his final eight months of life to do this. His courage and strength offered others a chance to be part of his personal journey, and the outpouring of love and support he received from friends and colleagues, and even acquaintances, helped him realize the impact he had made on others. He was able to acknowledge people's heartfelt gratitude in a way he hadn't prior to that time. In his journey toward death, those connections and conversations allowed my father to receive the gift of knowing how valuable he'd been to others.

• • • •

THE FIRST YEAR after you've lost someone can be particularly difficult. You experience all the firsts without your loved one: the first Mother's or Father's Day, birthday, and annual holidays where their absence is especially poignant. I took these days as opportunities for contemplation and reflection. Everyone marks time differently, but finding a meaningful and personal way to remember your loved one is a powerful experience. In her book *Good Grief*, Deborah Coryell writes about "taking her dad with her" on the anniversary of his birthday after his death. She told stories that introduced her father to her clients and others she knew as she went about her day.

In the 1970s, my father had a bumper sticker on his car that read: HAVE YOU HUGGED YOUR KID TODAY? In the months before he died, he talked about how hugs are a validation from other human beings that we exist, that we are worthy of a hug. Several times during my mitzvah project, I'd receive or give a hug and then I'd share my father's feelings about hugs with that person. When my dad's birthday came around the year after he died, I had the opportunity to speak and lead my weekly Toastmasters meeting. I chose mourning and grieving as our meeting's theme, and its impact on the group was notable. Many people weighed in to share stories about people they had lost, and it was one of the most moving meetings we'd ever had. With the permission of the club, I also shared one of my father's slightly off-color jokes, which helped me break out of my box and loosen up after such a heavy theme.

In our western society, we tend to avoid talking about death as much as possible, and yet it is something each and every one of us experiences. When I spoke openly to people about losing my father, people suddenly felt comfortable to share their own losses. We need outlets to remember our loved ones, to tell stories about the people we have lost. Having opportunities to do this, whether they are prescribed or self-created, can be powerful and healing.

♥ *Share stories on special days in memory of your deceased loved one.*

Seek Someone Out to Offer Support

I SAW A woman at synagogue whom I'd met about a year earlier at a local park. I approached her to say hello and inquire how she was doing, reminding her of our meeting that day. I remembered her name and the fact that she had a dog, as well as some other details about her life. By the look on her face, she was touched that I had remembered so much about her.

• • • •

ANY OF US who live in a community will eventually run into people we know as we're going about our lives, whether at the grocery store or movies or elsewhere. We might make a conscious decision to avoid people, going down another aisle or somehow trying to dodge this face-to-face encounter. I've done this myself, for all kinds of reasons— whether I was short on time or wasn't in the mood to interact. However, you never know when this kind of an opportunity can make a difference for someone else. Based on the woman's expression in this case, this seemingly simple action of my approaching and connecting with her had a positive effect. Some of what I had remembered was that it had been a tough year for her. She'd gone through a hard divorce and was sorting her life out. Her response to our conversation told me she was grateful that I had listened and heard her when we met in the park that day. In this busy and chaotic world, having someone show understanding can create the moments of meaning in our lives.

♥ *Approach someone who needs your open heart and listen to them.*

Clean Up Your House of Worship

A FATHER APPROACHED me after synagogue to share that my seven-year-old son had cleaned up the kids' playroom without being asked. We shared a moment of understanding that these actions are worth acknowledging. I later told my son I was proud of him. I wanted to recognize him and told him I was proud to record his mitzvah.

• • • •

I'VE WRITTEN ABOUT how valuable positive feedback from another parent can be in other chapters. People who recognize our children's helpfulness can in turn help us take notice of moments in our children's lives that we might have otherwise missed. When my kids were little, we belonged to a cooperative playgroup. At one of the sessions, a little boy was going around and hitting all the other children. His mother was beside herself with embarrassment, and many of the other mothers with older children assured her that her son's behavior was a normal phase. Not a year later it was my son's turn. He went through a hitting phase, and suddenly I was the mom with a "challenging" child. I remembered those other mothers' words and felt grateful for all the mothers who had come before me, knowing I wasn't alone.

Around the time this mitzvah occurred, Hillary Rodham Clinton was running for president, and I heard her speak often about the fact that "It Takes a Village" to raise a child. Other adults play a vital role in how we raise our kids. Sometimes they are the primary caregivers in a day care setting. They may also be adults we encounter who acknowledge our kids themselves, or tell us about their good deeds, or sometimes sympathize with the more difficult aspects of what it takes to raise kids. Let's all remember that we don't have to raise our kids alone. The help, support, encouragement, and praise we receive from others along this parenting journey is essential. During the mitzvah project, I was not only aware of my own children's actions, but also the actions of other parents, including this dad who praised my son and those mothers who helped me realize that difficult phases impact every parent on the planet and that I wasn't alone.

♥ *Praise your child or someone else's child when they help out without being asked.*

Deliver Gifts of Food for Purim
and Other Holidays

THE ANNUAL FESTIVAL of Purim commemorates the freeing of the Jewish people from the Persian nobleman Haman, who was actively engaged in a plot to destroy them. The Megillah, or Book of Esther, is read each year to tell the story, and Jews dress in masks and costumes to celebrate this event, giving out gifts of food, providing charity to the less fortunate, and enjoying a celebratory dinner, the Feast of Purim.

In Judaism, there are 613 mitzvot that we are commanded to do. The following four are connected with our spring holiday of Purim: (1) *Mikra Megillah,* hearing the Megillah read; (2) *Seudah Purim,* enjoying a festive Purim meal; (3) *Mishloach Manot,* giving gifts to friends; and (4) *Matanot l'evyonim,* giving gifts of charity to the poor.

The mitzvah of giving to the poor is very specific. The act of giving, as well as the amount we give, reminds us that each of us is part of a larger community. The custom says that rich and poor alike must give an equal amount: three half-dollar coins. There is no differentiation between rich and poor. In this case, we are all considered the same and are encouraged to give our three half-dollar coins. The half-dollar is a symbolic amount that represents part of a whole.

The mitzvah of giving gifts to our friends has a practical aspect: to ensure that everyone has enough food to enjoy the Purim holiday feast. The second reason for this custom is to increase the feeling of friendship and love in the community. People also give gifts to friends, neighbors, teachers, and family members.

• • • •

WHILE I HAVE generally kept our gifts simple, some people make quite elaborate gift bags for Purim. Ours includes a juice box, peanut butter sandwich crackers, *Hamantaschen* (the traditional triangle-shaped Purim cookie), and some kind of chocolate. We have friends from the East Coast who still send us *Mishloach Manot* even though we haven't lived near them in years, and it's a wonderful gift to know that we're still in their thoughts and prayers even after all this time.

If you'd like to observe the gift basket custom on Purim, make a list of people in your life whom you would like to receive your gifts. While our family often gives to several close friends, we have also found it's fun to give gifts to friends and family who don't celebrate this custom.

Choosing to start a new custom in your life shouldn't be overwhelming. Perhaps you want to light candles for Shabbat, collect *tzedakah* to donate to a favorite charity, make a blessing before or after a meal, or deliver special treats on holidays. Whatever custom you decide to add to your life, find one that is meaningful and adds joy when you do it. For our family, this custom of giving *Mishloach Manot* makes us smile each and every year.

♥ *Start a new tradition in your household.*

Befriend a Newcomer

WE WERE INVITED to attend a bar mitzvah for a boy in our community, but on the morning of the celebration my kids weren't feeling well, so my husband stayed home with them and I went on my own. A half an hour after I arrived, a woman sat in the row in front of me. She seemed unsure of what to do, and it was immediately apparent that she was a non-Jewish guest. I leaned forward and told her what page we were on and she promptly got up and moved to sit next to me. She had a camera in her hand and I politely told her that taking photos during the service was not permitted. I continued to help her find her page and quietly answered a few of the questions she had about the service as we went along.

• • • •

SITTING NEXT TO someone who has likely never attended a bar or bat mitzvah before made me think about what the service must have felt like for her. I assumed it was difficult to follow along since the prayer book reads from right to left and most of it is in Hebrew. It reminded me of a similar experience I had while traveling in Spain when I followed a self-guided walking tour and stopped at a beautiful old church. I wandered inside and sat down. Not three minutes later, the priest came in and began to conduct services. I was so surprised that I just stayed put and tried to blend in (I'm sure unsuccessfully). Given that the mass was in Spanish, I couldn't follow along at all, and I felt pretty uncomfortable, as much as I tried to take it all in as an interesting experience.

Being unfamiliar with customs and rituals can be intimidating. This pertains not only to religious services, but to meetings or group gatherings, as well. It is always better to be greeted by a smiling stranger who helps you through the moments of disorientation, and

My Home Away from Home

who's approachable enough that you feel like you can also ask questions. Make it a new policy the next time there's a newcomer in your midst at a meeting or a service to welcome them and show them the ropes, whether you've been appointed to or not.

♥ *Greet and welcome a newcomer to your service, meeting, or event.*

Take on a New Job or Task

IN THE SPRING of 2009, my family and I decided to join a new synagogue after considerable discussion. I decided I wanted to be engaged in their community by doing something that would help the synagogue and its members. One of my college friends worked there, and she told me about a project that involved sending condolence cards to family members who had recently lost a loved one. Even though it had been two years since my dad died, I was still working on the mitzvah project and this seemed like a great fit for me. I was honored to be doing something for people whose experience I could relate to.

This undertaking was done on behalf of the *bikur cholim* committee. In Hebrew, *bikur cholim* means "visiting the sick," and it's a term that encompasses a wide range of activities performed by an individual or a group to provide comfort and support to people who are ill, homebound, isolated, and/or otherwise in distress. When my father died, a new young rabbi came by my house to make a visit even though I wasn't a member of his synagogue. When I mentioned this to him after expressing my gratitude, he said, "You are still a member of our community regardless of what synagogue you belong to." It was an amazing gift and made me realize that I did indeed have a connection to others through a larger community, and this was something I often thought about as I moved through my grief.

• • • •

INITIALLY, I ASSUMED I would enjoy this mitzvah. It seemed to be a chance for me to connect with the bereaved, and it was definitely in perfect alignment with the mitzvah project and honoring my father. The first cards were easy to write. I didn't know the recipients or the deceased, but I could relate to their grief and wrote the notes from my heart. Every week, I would receive an email in my in-box from the synagogue secretary with the subject line: "Deaths."

As the weeks went on, however, this mitzvah began to feel like a burden. It felt like a never-ending task, and what had initially been heartfelt started to feel more difficult with each passing week. I eventually asked to be relieved of my duties after several months of helping on this project. In this case, I didn't feel like I was giving up on something. I found it to be rewarding while it lasted, but at some point the reward turned into a heavy burden that was becoming a struggle. There are plenty of opportunities for mitzvah work out there, and my feeling is that you should feel passionate about what you do, even in your volunteering efforts.

♥ *If a volunteer opportunity isn't working out, don't be afraid to leave.*

Donate to a House of Worship

IN THE FINAL weeks of the mitzvah project, I received a request from an old friend whom I'd recently reconnected with on Facebook. He and I had met in the mid-1980s when we'd spent a year abroad together. His email was a plea for help. His childhood synagogue in Harrisburg, Pennsylvania, had suffered a tragic fire. I immediately sent money to help with the rebuilding efforts. I later found out that the rabbi of that synagogue had been one of our counselors during our year abroad. This was an unexpected connection that brought a smile to my face.

• • • •

IT'S PARTICULARLY MEANINGFUL to help a friend or acquaintance when they reach out with a personal request for help. When you've received requests for help from various causes, aren't you generally more motivated to get involved and participate when you know the person who's sending the request? Why is that? Because our connection to the person makes the request that much more personal, and it makes us feel like we're supporting someone we care about by giving to a cause or effort they care about. It's not an abstract occurrence. It now has a name and a face so it is closer to us. It compels us to get involved.

Fundraisers and volunteer coordinators know this, too. We tend to give more when we have a personal connection. This is good to keep in mind. Sometime in the future, if you or an organization you belong to are in need, don't hesitate to reach out and ask for support. People are often looking for ways to feel like they're making a difference. Don't assume you're burdening people with your request.

♥ *Make the personal connection when in need. Others will be drawn to help.*

CHAPTER 8

····

THE REUSABLE
BAG LADY

····

"When God created the first man, he showed him all the trees in the Garden of Eden and said, 'See how beautiful and perfect are my creations! All that I have created, I created for you. Therefore, be mindful so that you do not abuse or destroy my world. For if you abuse or destroy it, there is no one to repair it after you.'"

—ECCLESIASTES RABBAH 7:13

· environmental conscience ·

I NEVER PAID much attention to reducing, recycling, and reusing when I was growing up. But now, as an adult, and especially as a mother, I've often reflected how growing up in a rural community naturally fostered these philosophies. Living in a small town, population 1,200, and on quite a big piece of property by city standards, meant there were lots of opportunities for living off the land. Our farmhouse was located on seventeen acres. My parents raised dozens of animals, including horses, pigs, ducks, chickens, dogs, and cats—and we had a garden the size of an elementary school baseball diamond. We also had a compost pile that was bigger than the living room in the house I live in today. Barn sales were common, and people reused items as a way of life.

Soon after my brother and I went away to college, my parents relocated to Burlington, Vermont, the state's largest city. Since leaving Vermont, I've lived in several major cities. After my husband and I got married, we relocated to Portland, Oregon, a state whose progressive political and environmental views I cherish. I love living in a state where recycling is the norm and sustainability is a topic that gets a lot of coverage. We have a supermarket chain called New Seasons Market whose commitment to sustainability has set the standard for businesses. The chain has grown by a dozen stores since it opened ten years ago; it's not only weathered the economic downturn but has also flourished. Their commitment to serving and teaching about sustainability has helped educate thousands of people. I recently found out that when the store opened they had only one Dumpster for garbage and one for compost. Now they have two compost Dumpsters and one garbage Dumpster. I was excited to learn this because it shows that profitable businesses can have sustainable practices and help teach others, as well.

As people's awareness of our impact on the environment grows, more people are starting to think about their carbon footprint, and many of us are looking for things we can do to reduce our impact on the environment. Mitzvahs to the earth are a great way to do this! In Judaism, one of the important concepts of *tikkun olam,* or "repairing the world," has to do with social action concerning the environment. I find that small acts of kindness toward our environment do more than just improve the quality of everyday lives; they help make us feel like we're actually making a difference.

Change Your Habits

LIKE MANY AMERICANS, I frequent Starbucks. During the past seven years, while I ran a home-based business, I often met clients there. On many occasions I even visited two different Starbucks in one day. On the morning of this mitzvah, I was having coffee with a friend. As usual, when I asked for my drink, I asked for it in a "for here" glass (as in, not paper), since it's Starbucks' policy to automatically serve drinks in a to-go cup. My friend told me she usually doesn't think to order her drinks "for here," and she said I'd inspired her to remember to order it that way in the future.

• • • •

OLD HABITS ARE hard to break. If you become conscious of little actions you can take to use less and recycle more, it makes a difference. My friend was not in the habit of asking for a "real" cup at Starbucks, since she'd never given it much thought before. Our discussion reminded her that even if you don't do it every time, you can make choices to create less waste whenever possible. Who knows, Starbucks might have to change their policy and at least offer patrons a choice.

In recent years, there has been a push for customers to use their own reusable mugs, and more and more people seem to be doing that, too. Peet's Coffee and Starbucks both offer a ten-cent discount to patrons who bring their own mugs from home. The exchange with my friend reminded me of my favorite quote by Margaret Mead: "Never doubt that a small group of thoughtful, committed citizens can change the world; indeed, it's the only thing that ever has."

♥ *When staying at a coffee shop to have your drink, request it in a "for here" cup or bring your own.*

Create a Collection Point

A WOMAN AT a local synagogue in Portland organized a project to collect and recycle used fluorescent lightbulbs and batteries. This smart environmental mitzvah was very inspiring, and a lot of people commented on how valuable it was. I decided to write a thank-you note to the woman telling her how grateful I was that she was doing this project, and for providing a space for myself and others to take care of recycling our lightbulbs, which too many people simply throw away. This mitzvah was another woman's mitzvah, and it begat my mitzvah of recycling, too, making it easy for me to collect lightbulbs and batteries that were just sitting around my house waiting to be recycled.

• • • •

IF YOU ARE passionate about something, take action to get involved. This mitzvah only occurred because someone decided she wanted to help others properly dispose of their fluorescent bulbs and batteries. It prompted me and dozens of other people to make good choices in our own efforts to recycle. Perhaps you want to start a collection at your place of worship, office, or home. Not only will you be making a difference, your efforts will impact others and perhaps inspire them to do the same. Ghandi said, "Be the change you wish to see." Decide what you value and take the actions necessary to make it happen. Go be the change!

♥ *Start a recycling program at your home, office, or place of worship.*

Reuse Art Supplies

THIS MITZVAH IS one of my favorites. Donating two bags full of "potential art supplies" to SCRAP allowed me to unload things my kids were never going to use again, and it helped SCRAP out by replenishing their supplies. I have mentioned SCRAP in other chapters, but it's such an incredibly cool organization that it deserves to be discussed again here. SCRAP, the School and Community Reuse Action Project, is a Portland-based nonprofit organization that takes all sorts of items that you might normally throw away. The items are then reused in creative ways for art projects and home decor. This organization is helping to keep thousands of pounds of trash out of the landfills.

• • • •

UNTIL I LEARNED about SCRAP, I always bought brand-new art supplies for my kids. It turns out that they are just as happy to go to SCRAP and reuse items that would otherwise end up in the trash—and I couldn't be happier about that! The art projects are unique and incredibly creative. One year, my daughter applied corkscrews, old pieces of felt, leather, and some Popsicle sticks to a piece of wood to make a tepee and a Native American scene for a school project. Another year she made a sea grotto scene from *The Little Mermaid* out of many found items at SCRAP that were one-of-a-kind.

I heard a parent lamenting recently how short a lifespan school projects have, which is all the more reason to use items from places like SCRAP. The more we can find ways to reuse materials, the better. Kids are creative and have limitless ideas about how to use unusual supplies. While many options, like SCRAP, are opening up across the country, not every city has this kind of resource. However, schools, libraries, or community centers are generally open to considering ways they can be a hub to help recycle usable materials for their constituents. Ask in your community about starting a collection spot for this very same thing.

In first grade, both of my children participated in Imagination Station, a center set up by their teachers to make art projects out of recycled materials. The teacher was constantly looking for reusable items, and it was a win-win for everyone involved. I loved being able to "recycle" items from our house that I thought would make for interesting projects. Plus, the kids loved the station and brought home supplies to work on new projects at home. More schools could make use of this idea and create art programs out of found items rather than new materials. That certainly would make things cheaper and more environmentally friendly and would instill the message of recycling, reusing, and reducing.

♥ *Choose reusable art supplies for school and home projects.*

To the Dump

AFTER MY DAD died and I went on my nesting and organizing spree, I found many items to donate and others to recycle. I made several trips to the recycling center that spring. It reminded me of the many times I accompanied my dad to the dump as a teenager. We didn't have any sophisticated recycling opportunities back then, but plenty of people left still-usable items at the dump. We had a system in rural Vermont where people would leave usable items for others to take home in a designated section. We collected and dropped off small household items and plenty of furniture, over the years. Luckily, in my larger suburban town there are lots of wonderful recycling opportunities that make it easy to recycle all sorts of items. One organization, called Community Warehouse, takes usable household items and redistributes them to families in need. It's a hub for donations, and the donor knows their item is immediately helping someone else. Lots of people also capitalize on the ample opportunities available on websites like craigslist to pass on and acquire used stuff.

• • • •

SOMETIMES IT'S EASIER to throw our things in the garbage rather than collect the items and drive them to a recycling center. But every small action we take makes a difference—from carrying our bags to the store to recycling batteries and fluorescent lights to making monthly trips to the recycling center. I am a huge fan of craigslist, and I am continually amazed at how effectively you can connect with someone who's getting rid of the very thing you want, or with lots of people who want what you have! I have found a home for old lawn mowers, piles of bricks, and, of course, toys my children have outgrown. Sometimes, I can even make a few bucks.

What's easy to do is also easy not to do. Each action helps us pay attention to what we are using, consuming, and how our efforts can make a difference. It doesn't always seem like our small efforts will amount to anything, but each time I visit the recycling center, I am reminded that collectively they absolutely do.

♥ *Make the small effort to recycle. It does make a difference.*

Be the "Reusable" Bag Lady

AROUND 2006, MANY stores in the Portland area began carrying reusable bags. I jumped on the bandwagon that year by purchasing a few myself. Like all new habits, I initially found it hard to remember to bring my bags into the store. A few times I had to leave the checkout line to run back to my car for the bags. One time, my daughter suggested I put a sticker on my bag every time I reused it. She said it would show me how many times one bag gets used. I thought it was a great idea, but eventually I just got in the habit of keeping the bags in a more visible place so I would remember to bring them in with me when I went shopping.

• • • •

USING REUSABLE BAGS is my biggest good-earth mitzvah. What initially began as a new habit that I kept forgetting has turned into part of my everyday routine. I have several reusable bags, which is crucial when shopping for a family of four. The secret is to dump your groceries and then put the bags immediately back into your car. You might also want to keep them in the front seat until you are in the habit of carrying them into the store every time. Many stores in Portland now post signs asking if you remembered your grocery bags. Perhaps one benefit of this new environmental awareness is that kids aren't embarrassed by something being reused over and over again. My kids are proud of reducing, reusing, and recycling, and I know that by instilling these values at such young ages, they'll certainly carry them forward into their lives. Make a resolution to start carrying your own bags to the store. You'll be amazed at how easy it is to create this new habit.

While working on this chapter, I began consciously trying to reuse all my vegetable bags each week as well as bulk bags and canisters. There are reusable vegetable bags now available that help make this even easier.

♥ *Carry your bags to the grocery store. If you already do that, begin carrying your bags everywhere you shop!*

Lessons from Litter

MY SON, DAUGHTER, and I went for a walk to pick blackberries in a neighborhood park. My son saw a piece of garbage and picked it up. He said he wanted to make America beautiful. The rest of the way he continued to pick up litter, and we joined in, too, moved by his initiative to keep the path to our park enjoyable and clean for others.

• • • •

THIS MITZVAH REITERATED that we are sometimes the teachers and sometimes the student. I offer daily lessons to my children, and this time my son offered me a lesson. His noticing the trash on our walk allowed us to talk more about how each of us can take care of our environment. When I was a teenager, I remember noticing beer cans strewn along the road on the drive home. Even as a self-involved teen, I was bothered that people would throw cans out of their car windows rather than find a trash can to put them in. On one occasion, my father and I pulled over to pick them up, and we, too, talked about social responsibility, a life lesson that has impacted my own parenting. Now, twenty-five years later, my son and I are having that same conversation, and I can see the powerful influence my father played shining through in his grandson.

♥ *Today, pick up litter on the sidewalk, in your neighborhood, at the park, at a school, or wherever you see it.*

Recycle Even While You're Away

MY DAUGHTER AND I made it a point to carry our reusable bags with us during our Florida vacation, and especially through Disney World. Although we didn't use them every time, we did manage to use them *almost* every time. A few times when clerks asked about them, my daughter stepped forward to explain why we were carrying them and why it was important. In Portland, Oregon, carrying reusable bags is the norm, but based on our experience in Florida, I would guess that isn't the case all around the United States yet. Although some of the clerks eyed us as if we were from another planet, we did have a wonderful discussion with one cashier who told us she appreciated our efforts and voiced her wish that more people she encountered would do the same.

• • • •

SOON AFTER I started carrying my own bags to the grocery store, I learned about a compact reusable bag that folds up inside itself. It's small enough to put in your purse or pocket but strong enough to carry a full bag of groceries. They're called ChicoBags, and you can buy them online at www.chicobag.com. They were the secret to my ease in reusing bags. I always carry at least one in my purse, and over the years, I've often given them to friends as gifts. Order some for yourself and see how easy it is to reuse bags while you're going about your regular business. Use your compact bags for everything you buy—it's amazing how easy it is! My daughter enjoyed many of those conversations with the cashiers. It reiterated the fact that you can be an example to others through your actions.

♥ *Take your new compact reusable bags on vacation. Let others know the benefits of reusing their bags.*

THE REUSABLE BAG LADY

Spontaneous Recycling

ON NEW YEAR'S Day, we were still in Florida on that same family vacation, and I woke up early to get some much-needed personal time. I started by taking a walk to the clubhouse at my in-laws' subdivision.

After a little while, I passed two women and asked them if I was headed in the right direction. Although they were walking the opposite direction, they offered to show me where the clubhouse was. As we walked, they told me I wouldn't be permitted to enter the clubhouse without an ID, so they offered to get me in as their guest. We chatted while we walked, and once we got there we were shocked by the remains from the New Year's Eve party left in the ballroom from the night before. The cleanup crew had just arrived to clean tons of garbage, including party hats, streamers, and hundreds of empty bottles and cans. The women were appalled that the management was not recycling, so they decided to take what they could to the local recycling center. I offered to join them.

• • • •

IT'S SUCH A gift when one mitzvah turns into another mitzvah, and that happened often during this project. My serendipitous meeting with these two women turned into an opportunity for the three of us to recycle literally hundreds of bottles and cans. I told them about my mitzvah project and pointed out that their mitzvah of walking me to the clubhouse had led to the recycling mitzvah for all of us. What a great way to start the new year. I felt almost giddy coming home and telling my husband about my morning adventure.

♥ *Find out about recycling day programs offered by your city or town and volunteer to help out.*

CHAPTER 9

····

IN THE
DOGHOUSE

····

*"An animal's eyes have the power to speak
a great language."*

—MARTIN BUBER,
GERMAN JEWISH BIBLICAL
PHILOSOPHER (1878-1965)

· animals ·

MOST OF MY animal mitzvahs had to do with a single animal, and often with one of our own pets. For people who love animals, there is no shortage of mitzvahs to be done that revolve around animals.

Perhaps you want to consider finding a way to share your love of animals through an agency that works with animals in some way. Most communities have animal shelters or a humane society, and there are many organizations that specialize in animal protection. The volunteer opportunities can range from walking, grooming, or fostering an animal to being on speakers' bureaus, stuffing envelopes, or helping with fundraising events. Animal rescue agencies are wonderful places to volunteer because you know your time is helping to make a difference in the lives of animals.

In Boring, Oregon, about twenty-five miles from Portland, there is a training campus for an organization called Guide Dogs for the Blind. This is a satellite campus of their location in San Rafael, California, north of San Francisco. I've grown so fond of seeing individuals with their guide dog puppies training throughout the city. I have even known a few families who have participated in this wonderful opportunity to raise a guide dog. The families that host these dogs agree to raise and socialize the dogs for fourteen to eighteen months to prepare them for life as a service dog. It is not an easy task, but most of the families I've talked to have been thrilled to help an individual out by raising a dog that will bring them independence.

Try to Rescue a Lost Dog

MY SON AND I were driving in a busy urban part of downtown when we saw several people crowded outside of a coffee shop pointing at a dog running loose through the streets. Since we were in the car, we were able to follow the dog down a few streets and through two different parking lots. We even pulled over twice in an attempt to call out to the dog, but he only looked back toward us and kept running. He was wearing tags, so we guessed he had just gotten loose. In the end, he got away from us and we weren't able to get him back to his owner. Of course, we never learned what happened to the dog.

• • • •

AT DINNER THAT night, my son and I told our story to my husband and daughter. An interesting discussion ensued. My son and I felt that our intention was to perform a mitzvah since we had followed the dog with the hope of helping him and returning him to his owner, but my daughter and husband didn't feel this counted as a mitzvah since we hadn't succeeded in catching the dog. This posed an interesting question for me. If you intend to help someone or something by doing a mitzvah but aren't able to complete it, have you still performed a mitzvah?

According to the Talmud, the Jewish collection of Jewish law and thought, if someone has the intention of doing a mitzvah and was for some reason thwarted from actually doing it, then the attempt alone is accepted as if it were the act (Kiddushin 40a). Here, the mere intention to perform a mitzvah is counted as if the mitzvah were fulfilled. My son and I concluded that doing a mitzvah or ritual with *intention*, which we had done in this case, did indeed count.

Several months later, my daughter and I found ourselves returning home one night when we saw a black Labrador dog running through

IN THE DOGHOUSE

our neighborhood. This time, we were able to stop the car and catch the dog in a neighbor's driveway. We knocked on the family's door. The Lab wasn't theirs, but it belonged to their backyard neighbors. The gentleman took the dog inside and said he would give the owners a call and get the dog home. Clearly this time we felt that our efforts had resulted in a mitzvah completed.

♥ *Return an animal to its owner if you can!*

Scoop Your Poop

ATTENTION ALL DOG owners: Scoop the poop! My son and I rode our bikes to the park at the end of our neighborhood to find that a dog had left a little present under the swings. This park, like many in our city, has doggie poop bags available from a dispenser. I quickly walked back to the entrance of the park to grab a bag, and picked up the poop so that no one else would accidentally step in it.

• • • •

WE HAVE BEEN dog owners for more than fifteen years, and it's a pet peeve of mine when dog owners don't clean up after their dogs! Over the years, I have certainly picked up my share of dog poop. When I have forgotten my own bags for cleanup, I have been known to knock on a neighbor's door to ask for a bag, or to find something on the street I can use to scoop. Never in all of my years of knocking on neighbors' doors have I had a neighbor upset with me for bothering them. In fact, it's the opposite; they're amazed and delighted that I am not just going to walk away and leave the poop for them to deal with. Next time you decide to walk away from your dog's mess, please think again and get creative. If you have forgotten a bag, which happens to all of us, look for another way to get an extra bag, perhaps another dog walker. There's no excuse for leaving your dog's mess. This simple action is not only an act of kindness, but it also will potentially save a stranger from an unexpected and unhappy occurrence.

♥ *Clean up after your pet, even if it means returning to the location to do so!*

Donate in the Aftermath of Losing a Pet

OUR FIRST DOG, a male Cavalier King Charles named Porter, died soon
after we returned from a vacation and just five months after my father
died. We had gotten him when he was eight weeks old, before both of
our kids were born. It wasn't a complete surprise when he died since
he'd been under the care of a cardiologist for the previous year, but that
didn't make the loss any easier. Because I was still mourning the loss
of my father, losing Porter just a few months later reopened the deeper
place of that grief. I was so grateful to all of the family and friends who
sent cards or called to extend their thoughts about our loss. I received
those cards and was touched that friends had reached out to connect. I
wanted to do something to turn this sadness into a mitzvah, so I gathered up all of Porter's unused pet food and medication and gave it to
the cardiology clinic where Porter had been getting treatments. I also
sent thank-you notes to all of the people who'd helped us raise Porter.

• • • •

PETS PLAY SUCH a vital role in our lives, and when they die it is devastat-
ing. The house can feel empty, and their absence can be not only sad
but also unsettling. Porter was the first animal I had ever raised and lost,
and his death coming so close on the heels of my father's death was
particularly intense.

I sheepishly shared how sad I was feeling with my rebbetzin on one
of our morning visits. I figured she might not understand, or make me
feel that my grief for an animal was silly. But she immediately put me at
ease and shared her own story about losing their dog many years before
and how she had cried for a week. Her sharing made me feel so much
better—and normal for what I was going through.

After Porter died, I wrote a note to our breeder, an amazing, caring, and compassionate person, thanking her for the years of help she had given us. She'd answered our endless questions and always gave us advice when necessary. In the end, I wanted her to know how much she had also impacted our lives. She offered to bury Porter at her home, and we were grateful for this unbelievable offer.

Giving Porter's medicine to the cardiology clinic was an obvious choice, but there are many outlets ready and grateful to take your pets' old things. Local shelters are generally prepared to receive dog medication, food, treats, toys, and beds that are all still in usable condition after a pet dies. When you are ready, don't be afraid to pass these items along. It was actually helpful for me to know that Porter's things would be used by another animal.

The process of sending thank-you notes and donating my dog's food and medication gave me a feeling of closure that helped me move forward after his death.

♥ *Acknowledge the death of a pet with thank-you notes and any appropriate donations. If you know someone who has lost a pet, send a pet condolence card.*

Have a Fundraiser

ONE SPRING WEEKEND, my daughter and her friend decided to set up a lemonade stand to raise money for the Oregon Humane Society. In addition to homemade lemonade and cookies, they also sold pencils they had decorated. This was the second year in a row she and her friend wanted to do this. The previous year they raised eleven dollars. It was fun to see the way they changed things up the second year. They enlisted the help of my son and some of the other kids in the neighborhood. They worked for almost three hours, yelling, waving, and jumping around to get people's attention. Many people stopped and bought their lemonade and cookies, and some even gave them extra money for the cause. One mom came back and gave them an extra five dollars because she was a dog lover. The girls raised thirty dollars that day, and they were so proud of their efforts. My daughter decided she would add in the money she'd been collecting each Friday night in her *tzedakah* can, and the grand total for OHS turned out to be over sixty dollars.

• • • •

THIS WAS ANOTHER of those proud moments during my mitzvah project. I have fond memories of my own lemonade stands as a kid, but it never crossed my mind back then to raise money for a charity. Since the girls had collected money for OHS, I called and arranged a drop-off time so that the girls could deliver their money directly and have some interaction with someone from the agency. It took almost two months until we finally got to deliver the money, but it was a wonderful opportunity and was definitely worth the wait. The educational coordinator gave the kids an hour-long behind-the-scenes tour where they got to hold cats and dogs and learn more about the facility. Talk about a good way to promote a cause and cultivate future donors! The coordinator's

effort and time helped the children realize the value of their donation and how their efforts were going to the direct care of the animals.
Encourage your children to come up with creative ways to help a cause
they care about.

♥ *Encourage a lemonade stand, bake sale, garage sale, or any other
kind of sale where the proceeds go to your childrens' favorite charity.*

Donate Money to a Doggie
Rescue Organization

I BUY OUR dog food and treats at a local pet store, a neighborhood place where the employees enjoy helping and answering questions as well as providing excellent customer service. Like many stores, they have coin canisters for donations at the checkout, and I often put in my change because I know they are helping animals in my neighborhood, and I want to support that.

• • • •

I HAVE MENTIONED these kinds of coin canisters in a prior chapter about donations. When you see these cans now, you might think more about how much good your small change is doing. These canisters also help give visibility to organizations that are seeking to help and protect our animals.

Growing up in Vermont, we owned many animals. My dad and stepmother were crazy about animals. During my teenage years, we had three dogs, five cats, two pigs, two geese, two ducks, and a bunch of chickens. My children have only ever had a dog, but having a pet has certainly enriched their lives. My daughter is already a huge animal lover, even though she went through a period when she was younger when she was afraid of dogs. Being able to give small change to make sure that other animals are helped and rescued is probably the easiest and simplest way to give of ourselves and to help our four-legged furry friends. Encourage your kids by giving them a few coins to drop into these canisters, as well.

♥ *Give your change to a local animal rescue organization.*

Pay Attention to Missing Animal Signs

A FEW DAYS before an unexpected snowstorm hit our area, I had noticed a sign for a missing cat at the end of the block. The cat was a tabby like one we had when I was growing up. Two days later, as I was getting over a cold and not wanting to trudge out in the slush, our six-month-old puppy, Ginger, was nudging me for a walk.

We hadn't gotten very far when I heard the mewing. It was very loud, and the cat was definitely trying to get my attention. I wasn't sure where it was coming from, but when I stopped and looked around, I saw a tabby cat sitting in my neighbor's tree house. I walked around to the front door and knocked. I asked the woman who answered if she owned a cat. She did not. I told her I thought I might have found a missing cat, and she helped me by coaxing him down out of the tree house while I went back to the sign to get the number. It turned out that Murray the cat had been missing for two nights, and his owner was beside herself with worry that he wouldn't survive the snowstorm. My neighbor and I were both heartened when Murray was happily reunited with his owner.

• • • •

AS A PET lover, there is no greater thrill than knowing an animal is safe and loved. Helping a lost animal get home gives a tremendous sense of relief because you can empathize. This mitzvah was special because it connected three neighbors. There was a real sense of community when we worked together to help unite Murray and his owner. Plus, the sheer relief and joy she expressed was priceless. You don't always get the happy ending in a situation like this, so when you do it is all the more gratifying.

♥ *Pay attention to missing dog and cat signs. You might be part of their happy reunion.*

Take Your Dog Visiting

IN THE MIDDLE of winter, I decided to bring our dog, Ginger, for a visit to the rebbetzin's house. Ginger was already two years old at the time, but she was still full of puppy energy. Luckily, she weighs less than twenty pounds, so even with all her exuberance, she wasn't too much of a nuisance. She ran through the house sniffing and exploring, bringing her youthful energy to the home. The rebbetzin held her and pet her, and in the end I am not sure whether Ginger or the rebbetzin enjoyed the visit more.

• • • •

SINCE THE 1970s, community programs have been bringing animals and people together for companionship. Animals are known to have tremendous benefits for the elderly, and they're often used in pet therapy in long-term care facilities. There are many benefits of pets visiting with seniors, and the effects range from diminishing emotional pain and physical pain to reducing anxiety and boredom.

After taking Ginger to visit with the rebbetzin, I realized that even though Ginger hadn't been trained as a therapy dog, she still could be a beneficial visitor to a long-term facility. As part of my daughter's preparation for her bat mitzvah, she decided to volunteer with Ginger at a Jewish long-term care facility in our area. Ginger is small enough that most of the residents were happy to pet her and hold her. We were even invited to a Doggone Pet Tea a couple of months later where Ginger was the special guest of honor. It was fun hearing the residents reminisce about their own animals and tell stories about their pets.

♥ *Find a local retirement community, hospital, or special education school that will let you bring in your well-behaved dog.*

CHAPTER 10

....

WHAT GOES
AROUND COMES
AROUND

....

"Don't worry that children never listen to you; worry that they are always watching you."

—ROBERT FULGHUM,
*ALL I REALLY NEED TO KNOW
I LEARNED IN KINDERGARTEN*

· teachable family moments ·

ECOMING A PARENT is one of the most rewarding and awesome life experiences we can have. When you hold your newborn in your arms, you are in complete awe at the new life you have created. You realize the vast responsibilities that come with caring for a child. The life lessons you want to impart to your kids will come up time and time again as you raise them from infancy to childhood and into adolescence and adulthood. We go from worrying about teaching them survival skills like how to feed, clothe, and shelter themselves, to introducing values that we may feel are intrinsic to them becoming good and happy people, like how to be compassionate and generous, and how to live a good life.

What you might not think about immediately, however, is what your children will teach you. Every parent knows the sheer delight when you become the student and your child suddenly and miraculously becomes the teacher. I had dozens of these moments while working on the mitzvah project—like the time my son and I chased a dog in our car through the city streets of Portland trying to catch him and get him back to his owner and the ensuing conversation about what constitutes a mitzvah, or when my kids initiated their own mitzvahs, cleaning up after people or offering their small kindnesses in ways that touched other people.

When I was a teenager, my father and I had serious differences, but even during those years, I know I taught my father a lesson or two. In my junior year of high school, my basketball team had a fundraiser to earn money to go to the girls' championship basketball tournament. We sold maroon and white plastic booster seat cushions that had our team logo on one side and local merchant advertisements on the other. My father was bowled over that somehow I'd convinced parents from the opposing team, whose team colors were green and gold, to buy our seat cushions. He said I had an entrepreneurial spirit. He shared this story for years, boasting about how creative, ingenious, and clever I had been in convincing the parents that the team logo and colors weren't the important thing—it was their comfort. My husband even remembers my father sharing this story when they first met. What stands out to me now is how, in the midst of a challenging stage of child rearing, my father clung to a moment of joy and delight that I had given him.

When I began my mitzvah project, I hadn't given much thought to the ways in which it would impact my children and our family life. Ultimately, it provided a jumping-off point for numerous family discussions about what counted as a mitzvah and how our actions affect ourselves and others. In addition to the many things I learned from my kids, there were also plenty of times when I just sat back and enjoyed their sharing, when they'd let me know about something they'd done that they thought or hoped would count as a mitzvah.

Return Something You Know
Belongs to Someone Else

AFTER SCHOOL, THE day before spring break, I accompanied my daughter and her friend to the school's lost and found. They were hoping to find anything they might have accidentally lost during the school year. While they were searching, my daughter's friend recognized a winter coat that belonged to a boy in their class. My daughter asked if they could run it out to him, as they knew he would still be waiting in line to catch the bus home. They eagerly ran out to reunite him with his coat, and were giggling and excited afterward.

• • • •

THIS MITZVAH IS proof that some kids are keen observers and pay attention to their surroundings. The girls immediately noticed that one jacket among the entire rack of clothing belonged to one of their classmates. Perhaps this awareness comes more easily to children than adults because they have less distraction in their lives, but regardless, the ability to be aware and pay attention to the little things is a wonderful lesson many adults could learn. The girls' ability to pay attention and be keen observers helped return something lost to a boy who surely would be missing his winter jacket.

It goes without saying that many of us are so busy and caught up in our own lives that we can barely find the time to pay attention to someone else's life. The idea behind taking time to smell the roses means a lot of different things, including taking the time to notice that someone may have dropped something, or that someone has left something behind, and returning it to them. I was pleasantly surprised when the girls not only recognized that something belonged to a boy in their class, but that they also had the wherewithal to run out and find him to return it to him. The girls were equally delighted by their own simple act of kindness.

♥ *Pay attention to other people. If they've dropped or lost something, return it to them.*

Share Your Passion with Your Children

IN SEPTEMBER, I organized a new fundraiser for our elementary school that raised a considerable amount of money for our Parent Teacher Organization (PTO). It was an entertainment booklet sale, which required students to go to their neighbors, family, and friends and take orders for the twenty-dollar entertainment booklets, which included discounts to various local establishments. As the coordinator, I picked up the kids' orders, completed the paperwork, and filled the orders. At the end of the sale, each student who participated got a small prize, and the student who sold the most booklets overall was rewarded with a gift card from Target.

• • • •

AS A NEW PTO member, I suggested a fundraiser that hadn't been tried for several years at our school. At first, the PTO board was not interested in the idea, but when I committed to chairing the event, they voted to support it. Running a fundraiser—whether it's a cookie dough or wrapping paper sale, a fun run, auction, or another special event—entails a great deal of volunteer hours.

My children loved the idea that I would actually be running one of the fundraisers at their school. They were excited that we would have access to the entertainment booklets, and they volunteered to collect the orders each day after school and distribute the prizes to all of the kids at the end of the two-week event. The day I showed up to kick off the event, I noticed that my kids even seemed a bit pretentious, gloating to their friends that I'd be supplying the entertainment booklets. Their excitement, however, translated into enthusiasm for the sale. They spent several afternoons walking our neighborhood and ended up as the high salespeople for our school that year. They were elated about their Target gift cards.

Our actions speak louder than our words. Our children watch as we get involved and hear our passion about what we care about. My children took that enthusiasm and magnified it when they went door-to-door selling the booklets and raising money for their school while I cheered them on.

♥ *Share your passion with your children and inspire them to have passions of their own.*

Say a Prayer for the Sick

AFTER THE JEWISH holiday of Yom Kippur, I mentioned to my family that our rabbi had shared an idea for an easy mitzvah we could do to say a prayer of recovery and renewed health whenever we saw an ambulance passing by. In the next few days, I saw a couple of ambulances pass and used that opportunity to say a silent prayer. Many days after Yom Kippur had passed, my son heard an ambulance and turned to me and said, "Mommy, did you say a prayer?" I was moved that he had remembered this mitzvah, and struck by the fact that the idea stuck with him even after the holiday had passed.

• • • •

WE HEAR SO many messages in our daily lives about things we *should* do. There is always something we could do better and should pay attention to, but that pressure can also be overwhelming. For some reason, the idea to say a prayer for someone who is passing in an ambulance resonated with me. Perhaps it had to do with the fact that I'd started the mitzvah project as an act of remembrance; perhaps it was because I am scared of hospitals and everything medical and never want to be in an ambulance being rushed to the hospital in an emergency situation. Regardless, I started practicing this mitzvah whenever I saw a passing ambulance with its siren blaring. What was more amazing to me, however, was that this clearly resonated just as much with my son.

In Judaism, we say a prayer called the *Mi Sheberakh* each day at services when the Torah is read for those in our community who are ill. We recite out loud the names of all people, whether they are family, friends, or community members. I have always found this prayer moving because I believe it allows us to take a moment to send out healing prayers for those who need them. I admit that I sometimes can't remember who to name and will often think of someone I should have named after the service has ended. On the other hand, this is often the place where the community learns that people are sick, and it provides an opportunity for us to reach out by sending a card, making a call, or visiting someone who might need some get-well wishes or more.

Here is the *Mi Sheberakh* prayer:

May the One who blessed our ancestors, bring blessings of healing upon *(recite the English or Hebrew name). May the Holy One mercifully restore them to health and vigor, granting them a healing of body and a healing of spirit. And may they be healed along with all those who are in need. Blessed are You, Lord our God. And let us say: Amen.

In the months before he died, my father told me he was certain that the prayer circle his Wednesday morning group made in his honor helped sustain him. He said, "I could feel their love and support all the time." It's hard to quantify how much a prayer can help another person, but for me that simple silent prayer when I hear an ambulance is a reminder not to take my life or my children's lives for granted and do my part in providing prayers for another human being, even ones I don't know.

♥ *Say a silent prayer when you hear an ambulance siren, or on behalf of someone who is ill.*

Keep a Watchful Eye Out for Other Kids

MY DAUGHTER'S BEST friend was waiting after school for her mom. Her mom sometimes runs late, so initially I didn't think much about it. However, as we pulled out of the school parking lot, I had a hunch that something was amiss, so I called her mom to double-check. It turns out that several pieces of information had not been relayed, and her daughter should have gone home with another child after school. I turned around and went back to pick her up. I intended to drive her home, but the girls begged for a last-minute playdate, which we quickly arranged.

• • • •

MY BIRTH PARENTS were incompatible for many reasons, but one thing in particular that stands out for me about their differences was that my mother was punctual, never arriving late for anything, while my father was habitually late. For years, when we arranged visitation hand offs, my mother would be frustrated that my father still couldn't seem to show up on time.

I'm punctual like my mother, and as a result, our family always runs on time or before schedule. One year, when my daughter was about four, she stayed with my parents while I accompanied my husband on a business trip to Holland. The day after we returned, I was still jet-lagged, and I fell asleep while my daughter was at preschool. I never heard the alarm go off or the call from the preschool to see why I hadn't arrived to pick up my daughter. I woke up in a panic and rushed to the school arriving a half hour after our regularly scheduled pickup time. Even though this was such an unusual occurrence, to this day my daughter still talks about the time I left her at school. As any parent knows, kids will remember our mistakes.

Just like we don't want to dwell on the things our children have done wrong, it's also important that our children notice the things we do right. My daughter called this after-school pickup of her friend a mitzvah (probably because she got a playdate out of it), but my son said doing something like picking up a friend isn't a mitzvah because it's something we are supposed to do. It was interesting to hear their banter about this on the car ride home and to realize how invested they'd become in the mitzvah project.

♥ *Set an example for your children with your actions. Have discussions with them when your example falls short.*

Validate Your Child's Feelings

BEFORE THANKSGIVING, MY son had his hair cut by a local hairdresser. He despises getting his hair cut, and if it were up to him, he would never get it done. I have taken him to several stylists and he has often left in tears. We finally found a stylist who was extremely patient and listened to everything we asked her to do. She did exactly what my son told her and gave him a haircut we both could live with. The following week, we stopped by to thank her.

• • • •

AS A PARENT there are constant decisions to make on behalf of your children. Over the years, I have learned that some things are worth fighting over and some just aren't. There were plenty of times when I'd simply stepped in on my son's behalf and told a stylist what I wanted, leading to a meltdown. He'd leave in tears and be very upset by the experience. Finally, I realized that he needed to have a say in his hairstyle.

With the right stylist, we were able to have an experience that made us both happy. I was shocked by the overwhelming feeling of gratitude I had for the stylist who had taken the time to listen to my son, and who had worked to find a haircut we both loved. I also realized the importance of my son's feelings about his own appearance, and that he was getting to the age where what he wanted (at least where his hair was concerned) overrode what I wanted. In this instance, my son taught me a valuable lesson, as did this stylist. I felt it was imperative to let her know how much we appreciated her patience and kindness toward us, and it made me realize how important it is to validate our kids and let them know that they're being listened to.

♥ *Really listen to your children and decide if their request is possible.*

MITZVAH 550

Be Responsive When People
Ask for Advice or an Opinion

DAYS BEFORE CHRISTMAS, my children and I ventured into our local Costco. I made a point of letting the kids know we were only getting what we truly needed. As usual, Costco was packed and noisy, and I did my best to keep focused on getting in and out as fast as possible. A mom nervously approached my daughter and asked if she would mind trying on a pair of mittens to see if they would fit her daughter, whom she guessed was about the same age as mine. My daughter glanced at me for approval, and with my nod said she was happy to. My daughter reviewed for the mom which ones were the most comfortable and recommended the ones she liked the best. My son leaned over to me while my daughter was giving her advice and said, "Be sure to write that on your blog, Mom!"

· · · ·

DON'T TALK TO strangers! It's a common refrain parents tell their children. It's part of that protection we feel as parents to make sure our children stay safe. My daughter was clearly a little hesitant when this mom approached her, but seeing my nod allowed her to engage this woman and help her out with a legitimate request. My daughter was proud and excited to be asked to give her opinion. Many times adults don't care what a child thinks. Giving our children an opportunity to have an opinion is very powerful.

A few years ago, our school district announced budget cuts that would affect our school dramatically. Our school was in jeopardy of major cutbacks that would result in physical education, music, and library teachers being scaled back to half-time positions. A young girl in my son's third-grade class wrote a letter that she ended up reading at the budget committee's listening session to voice her opinion of the situation. I wasn't at the meeting, but I heard that she did an incredible job and was eloquent beyond her nine years. If we are to teach our children to stand up for what they believe and voice their opinions, it is crucial that they flex this muscle while they are children.

I loved seeing my daughter try on the mittens and suggest to the mom which ones would be the best choice. The mom loved her advice, too, and ultimately bought the ones she recommended. Watching my daughter have an opportunity to help someone and voice her opinion, even if it was as simple as which gloves to choose, showed me once again how important it is that we allow our children the chance to share what they know or think.

♥ *Provide opportunities for your children to step up and give their opinion or advice.*

Visiting the Hospital

A TEACHER MY son and daughter both had was in the hospital after a foot surgery, and we decided to go visit him after school one day, along with one of my daughter's friends. My daughter was apprehensive about going to the hospital and worried about seeing her teacher in a hospital bed, but it wasn't as scary as she had anticipated. He was sitting up in bed when we arrived, not looking like a patient. There were no IVs hooked up or any other kinds of hospital equipment visible. A few minutes later, the nurse asked the kids, "Can I get you guys some ice cream?" "Yes!" they screamed.

• • • •

KNOWING MY DAUGHTER was particularly nervous about what condition her teacher would be in (no doubt in part to my own dread of hospitals), I tried to prepare her for what she might see. We talked about why a person might have tubes attached to their hand or their nose. It's not easy for anyone, especially children, to see someone they care about out of their normal routine and looking ill. But how else do children learn about the realities of life if they never see anyone who is in the hospital or ill?

I knew it was an important visit both for their teacher and for my kids. As we left the hospital, my daughter said, "Mommy, usually I don't like to look around too much, especially into the other hospital rooms because you never know what you'll see. This time, though, I felt brave enough to do it." We can overcome our fears. My daughter did that day at the hospital and taught me that sometimes we have to step through our fears and see what happens. Oftentimes our children are role models to us as they embrace their fears and push forward anyway.

♥ *Visit a family member or friend in the hospital.*

Be a Role Model for the Children

MY MOM GOT free passes to a preview of the Disney movie *High School Musical*, and she and my kids were fired up for their special school night excursion. The local Disney radio station was going to be at the event giving away tons of gifts—T-shirts, hats, megaphones, banners, and pom-poms. Volunteers were throwing the gifts into the audience, and we never seemed to be in a position to catch one. My kids settled in and were satisfied getting to watch the preview just the same. After the movie, the kids were animated while discussing their favorite songs and parts of the movie. We followed another family of four with their grandparents out of the theater, their hands full of prizes. Somehow this family had scored two T-shirts, two megaphones, and two pom-poms! As I was pondering how they could have managed to score such a huge number of prizes, the mother reached out and ripped two more banners off the glass doors to add to their loot. Immediately, I started fuming and all I could think of was what an awful role model she was for her two kids.

About fifty feet outside of the theater, the boy dropped a plastic spoon he was carrying and proceeded to walk away, leaving his litter for someone else to pick up and throw away. I was so irritated with this family that I picked up the spoon and called to the son and told him he dropped his plastic spoon and that it needed to be thrown away. I left it at that, although part of me was screaming to do more.

I hadn't said anything to my kids about this family, but when we got to the car, my daughter asked, "Mommy, how did that family get so many prizes?"

"I don't know," I answered. Her question made me think of an idea, though, so I drove back around and parked in front of the theater. My kids and my mom stayed in the car while I walked back inside to ask the manager, "Can I have the last two banners on the entrance door for my kids?"

"I don't see why not," she said, and took them down and handed them to me.

"Did you ask permission for those?" my daughter questioned me when I got back to the car. "Yes," I assured her.

• • • •

NOT ONLY DO our children see what we do, they see what other people do. My kids instinctively knew that this family with all the prizes hadn't behaved in an exemplary way. We can't change someone else's behavior, but we can certainly use other people's actions as teaching moments with our children. Ironically, I didn't need to say or do anything this night. My children saw it all for themselves. They let me know that even at nine and six, they knew right from wrong and were sure to keep me in line to do the right thing, too.

♥ *Act as a role model for your own children and other children.*

Encourage Your Children's Initiative

WE INVITED SOME friends over for dinner at the last minute, and I had no idea what I would make for dessert. I opened the pantry and saw a holiday gift we'd received from my son's teacher a few months before: sand art brownies. This simple gift included all the dry ingredients to make chocolate brownies—all ready to go in a Mason jar. All I needed to do was add eggs and oil and bake! We threw the whole dessert together in less than ten minutes and they were absolutely scrumptious—not to mention beautiful, since they actually look like layers of sand. After dinner, I told my son he should send his teacher a note and tell her how easy and delicious her brownies were, and how we'd used them for a dinner party to share with friends. A few minutes later he disappeared to his room and came down a little while later with a very sweet thank-you note.

• • • •

THIS WAS ONE of those moments when my son showed me not only how truly capable he is, but how much initiative he has, too. There are plenty of times when I ask my kids to do something and they either just don't get around to it or forget. But this time my son clearly felt moved to get on the ball right away, and didn't feel the need to dictate to me, or to copy the words I told him to write; he came up with all of it on his own. When my son returned with his note in hand, I was amazed by how much thoughtfulness he had conveyed in the card. At an instinctual level, children are full of lessons for adults about how to live in gratitude and joy more often.

♥ *Praise your children when they do the right thing.*

CHAPTER 11

····

EXPRESSIONS OF GRATITUDE

"I can no other answer make, but, thanks, and thanks."

—WILLIAM SHAKESPEARE

· a hundred ways to say thank you ·

I N OUR COUNTRY, a lot of people experience Monday morning blues. They drag themselves to jobs they hate and spend their days getting through the week. On some Monday mornings during the mitzvah project, I sat down to write a thank-you card, or made a phone call first thing, seeing it as an answer to the Monday morning blues. It worked perfectly. Starting your week with some gratitude and appreciation trickles into the rest of your day and week, and it's a great practice to get into.

Thank-you cards and phone calls are opportunities to take time each day to give gratitude. They offer us a chance to tell someone else that they matter to us and to let them know why. In Judaism, we're encouraged to say one hundred blessings a day. We might say them upon waking up, ritually washing our hands, before and after eating, lighting candles, upon seeing a rainbow, and when we have reached a special moment in time, to name just a few.

In addition, the *Shacharit* morning service has a central prayer called the *Shemoneh Esreh* or *Amidah*, which is divided into three sections of blessings. One part expresses our thankfulness to God, another makes requests (for health, prosperity, forgiveness, etc.), the third simply praises God.

At certain times in my life, I have been more successful at this practice of saying daily blessings. While attending a Jewish summer camp and during my year abroad in Israel, I was more into the practice because I was living in an environment that truly supported it every day. However, even now when I don't recite prayers consistently every day, I have been known to suddenly burst out with the *Shehecheyanu* prayer, or what I like to think of as the gratitude prayer. Here is the prayer:

Blessed are You, Lord our God, Ruler of the Universe, who has granted us life, sustained us, and enabled us to reach this occasion.

The *Shehecheyanu* prayer gives us an opportunity to give thanks for reaching a special moment in time. Reciting this blessing can help you appreciate the little things happening in your life. This prayer is commonly said at the beginning of holidays, the birth of a child, a wedding, but also when you see a friend you haven't visited with in more than a month, or even when you buy a new article of clothing.

Living in a state of gratitude is a well-understood concept across many faiths. Mindfulness plays a central role in Buddhist meditation, and it is something to strive for to achieve enlightenment. If you are grateful for the things in your life, you will be more conscious of them; when you acknowledge the things you are grateful for, you will be in a state of deeper appreciation.

I remember years ago when Oprah invited her viewers to keep a gratitude journal. I was an exhausted, busy, stay-at-home mother and loved the chance to write down what I was grateful for each night. It also helped me realize how much I had in my life and not to take any of it for granted. Even on my most challenging days, I could easily include so many things. Recently, I attended a happiness seminar, and I learned that it isn't even important that we keep up with this practice every day. Keeping a journal by your bed and doing it once a week, a few times a week, or whenever you can is just fine. I've enjoyed going back and looking at the gratitude pages I kept from the years after my kids were born and the years after my father died, in part because I found that I was mostly grateful for the same exact things.

It is possible to find something to be grateful for every day no matter what your life circumstances. While writing this chapter, I read a quote from one of my favorite authors, Dr. Wayne W. Dyer: "Be an appreciator rather than a depreciator of everything that shows up in your life. Say, 'Thank God' for everything."

Thank-you notes are just a physical extension of our gratitude. I know the world would be a better place if anytime we were thinking about someone, we called or sent them a note to let them know they were on our mind. The year my dad died, there were several people who sent me condolence cards that surprised me. They were people I didn't know all that well and the fact that they took the time to send me a card to let me know they were thinking about me was very touching. The experience of receiving those cards made me realize that I could do the same thing, so making calls and sending thank-you cards became a big part of my mitzvah project.

I encourage you to have some blank note cards and stamps on hand so you can write your cards at the drop of a hat. Of course, when you give you also receive, and I have been the recipient of my share of heartfelt notes. If you want to help make the world a better place, this one simple practice could be an easy step to take.

Call upon an Elderly Neighbor

OFTEN DURING OUR busy lives, we forget to see how our elderly or homebound neighbors and family are doing. A quick phone call or drop-in can make all the difference. I called an elderly friend, a woman in her late eighties who used to teach piano to my husband. We chatted on the phone for a few minutes and arranged a time I could stop by during the next week.

• • • •

I LOVE TO call my rebbetzin, who's recently turned ninety, to see how she is doing. I can literally count on one hand the times our phone conversations have lasted more than a few minutes. It's not so much that I call to shoot the breeze or for a long conversation, but rather to let her know that I'm thinking about her. It's amazing how these short calls make us feel connected. Of course, it's not about the length of the call per se, but I bring this up because so many people don't make the call they're thinking of making because it seems like it might be a burden, or that they're not going to have enough time to be on the phone. It doesn't have to be that way. Taking a moment just to say hello and connect is what matters.

I often think about my elderly neighbors when there is extreme weather. If it's particularly hot or we have a huge snowstorm, I wonder how they are doing alone in their homes or apartments. These are perfect times to check in on a neighbor you aren't that close with. Give them a call or knock on their door with a pitcher of cool lemonade in the summer, or a Thermos of warm hot chocolate in the winter, and visit for a few minutes.

♥ *Call or visit an elderly or homebound neighbor to see how they are doing.*

Thank Someone for Their Help

I'D HAD THE support of two wonderful volunteers during the entertainment book fundraiser I chaired at my kids' school. After it was over, I sent them thank-you notes to share with them how much I'd appreciated their help on the event.

• • • •

AFTER COMPLETING THIS fundraiser, I thought about the people who had really helped me pull off the event. Sometimes when we volunteer to run an event, there really isn't anyone to thank us for our efforts. We do whatever we do to make a difference, and we may even need to take time to thank those other volunteers who helped us. The act of writing thank-you notes allows the gratitude you feel to trickle from your head, into your pen, and out into the world. That's why we must preserve the art of sending thank-you notes. With our ever-moving progression to online communication, receiving a handwritten note is even more meaningful these days.

While living in Vermont as a teenager, some of my closest friends were kids I met through my Jewish youth group, many of whom lived in upstate New York, several hundred miles from my hometown. I wrote letters daily to these friends and received dozens of letters back over those years. I'd often run to the mailbox to see who had written, and I cherished those letters since they were the lifeline to my teenage social life.

It's hard to believe that just twenty-five years ago, snail mail was the only option besides telephone. Kids today don't write letters to their friends, instead opting to text, IM, Facebook, or email. But it's not just kids. Hardly anyone sends handwritten letters anymore. But a handwritten personal note has an effect that email can never achieve. The long-lasting and tangible quality of sending and receiving handwritten notes can't be replaced by digital communication. Plus, saving your letters and notes allows you a way to revisit them in the future. I didn't realize until after my dad's death how much his handwritten correspondence would mean to me.

During college, I had a dear friend whose father passed away. I lament the fact that during that time I had just met my husband and was too busy in the newness of my blossoming relationship to really be present for my friend. Our friendship drifted after that point, and we lost touch for many years. After my father died, I began thinking about my college friend, and I felt sad that I hadn't been able to be a better companion. I realized the depth of her sorrow around losing her father after experiencing that loss myself. I dreamt about her one night and the next day, while looking through some old things, a letter she'd written to me years before literally fell into my hands. With tears in my eyes, I sat and read the letter that expressed her hurt and disappointment in me for not being there for her in the aftermath of her father's death.

I immediately went online and tracked her down. When I contacted her, she initially wasn't sure she was ready to reconnect with me, but when I wrote her that I had just lost my own father and asked her to forgive me for not being there during her loss, she told me she was ready to forgive me. We have spoken a few times since then, and it has been wonderful reconnecting with this old friend after all these years. Forgiveness requires two people, one who acknowledges that they made a mistake and the other to accept that apology. I was pleased knowing that this development occurred because of that handwritten letter I found in my closet.

♥ *Send a note to thank someone for their help.*

Thank Someone Who Impacted Your Life

IN 2008, THE founder of the company I was working for passed away. At that point, I had been an independent consultant for the company for almost six years, but I had only met the founder once. He was a company legend, beloved for his bright red glasses and his charismatic personality. He had envisioned a skin-care company that would use botanical ingredients and no petroleum products long before *organic* became a buzzword. He also provided women more opportunities to earn money through a home-based business. His son was a current vice president, so I sent a condolence card to him and shared with him how the company had positively impacted my life.

• • • •

IF YOU ARE like me, sometimes you come up with crazy ideas. I am not sure why I decided to send the son of the founder a note, but I was moved to do so. I didn't expect to receive a response from him, but just sending the card felt like an important thing to do. I'm sure this had to do with how much of an impact it made on me to receive cards and condolences after my father's death. I thought a card from a far-removed employee might help buoy him at this difficult time in his life.

These little moments we act on in our lives create the tapestry of who we are—so why not act on impulses that will positively affect others? We struggle in our day-to-day lives to find meaning and importance, and I believe that the simple act of reaching out—whether you call, send a card, email, or Facebook message someone—will have a positive influence all around.

♥ *Send a note to an old teacher, friend, mentor, or colleague, and let them know the positive impact they had on your life.*

Thank People Who Provide You with Professional Services

MY DAUGHTER WAS an apprehensive dental patient as a child. Going to the dentist with her was agonizing for both of us. One dental visit during the mitzvah project was particularly notable because our dentist suggested we get sealants, which meant we had to return for a non-invasive procedure. The dentist was *incredibly* patient and very kind with my daughter, working slowly and describing everything she needed to do. In the end, it turned out to be a very positive experience. I wanted to let the dentist know how much I had appreciated her kindness and sent her a note to say thank you.

• • • •

THIS CHAPTER IS all about the value of thank-you notes, and I've talked in other chapters about taking the time to recognize someone who has done a good job, even letting their supervisor know. Sometimes it's worth the extra effort to document that good job. Our dentist had taken care of my children for several years, and up until that point, I hadn't ever thanked her or let her know how much I appreciated her patience with my daughter.

This is one of those simple ideas that has a boomerang effect. By sending more thank-you notes and expressing your gratitude to people who have helped you, you in turn will attract more positive situations in your life. Just wait and see.

When people send you thank-you notes, don't throw them out, save them. Find a special bag, book, or box, and put all of these notes into it. You will be amazed by how those cards can help you on a difficult day. It can be a reminder that you are loved and have made a difference in other people's lives. A friend of mine who worked as a chaplain at a

EXPRESSIONS OF GRATITUDE

163

local hospital told me about a fellow chaplain who created her own bag for received thank-you notes and had called it her Bag of Love. What a wonderful way to visibly remember that what we do in this life matters to others. In case you forget how fabulous you are, you can always grab your Bag of Love to remind yourself.

♥ *Send a note to someone whose professional services you have used. Tell them what it was in particular that was so special.*

Send a Note to a Teacher

WE HAD A teacher who was going through a difficult time physically. He was struggling with the effects of diabetes and had to have several small operations in addition to adjusting to living with this disease. We'd visited him in the hospital (Mitzvah 651), and although he was back home, I'd heard that he was still having a rough time. I wrote a card letting him know how much he had meant to our family and giving him some encouragement.

• • • •

WE ARE ALL living in the same world with the same twenty-four hours in each day, but how we spend those hours, minutes, and seconds varies immensely from person to person and has a huge impact on our lives and the lives of others.

I have heard that teachers much prefer a heartfelt thank-you note with a thoughtful sentence or two from their student than any of the trinkets or candies they tend to receive as gifts. Make it a point to go above and beyond whenever you can to help your kids thank their teachers. Our teachers are not compensated nearly enough for all the work they do, so sending thank-you notes—and volunteering more in the classroom—are good ways to help our teachers know how much we value and support them.

♥ *Have your child write a thank-you note to their teacher or write one on their behalf.*

EXPRESSIONS OF GRATITUDE

Thank Someone for the Work They Do

WITHIN A THREE-MILE radius from my home, there are two automotive repair shops that put up inspirational messages on their billboards each week. One day the message for the week was, "Human dignity is more precious than prestige." It wasn't that this message spoke to me more than any others, but in that moment, I realized how often I had driven by these messages and they had subconsciously changed my mood. I often pass by and begin to smile or laugh or nod in agreement with whatever statement or quote has been posted. I have enjoyed these inspirational messages for years, and so on this day, I decided a thank-you was in order since I had benefited from these messages for so long. I looked up the automotive shop phone number and called the owner, who was surprised to receive the call, but was also glad I'd done so!

• • • •

MAYBE YOU OWN a business with a billboard outside. If so, perhaps you could adopt this message idea on your own board. Instead of only putting up messages about your services and prices, start finding inspirational messages and put them up on your billboard. It will allow you an opportunity to share your message with the world. You never know who is driving by and reading your sign and whose day you'll brighten. It's a quiet way to spread goodwill in the world.

If you work in an office, you can create an inspiration jar to replace your candy jar. To begin, put inspirational messages on pieces of paper inside your jar and set it on your desk. Colleagues can stop by and pick out a quote for the day. It just might reframe their mood or mind-set, and it's a lot healthier than the candy jar!

If you are the lucky benefactor of a business practice that really impacts you on a deep level, take time to let the owner know. Even after maintaining a blog for more than three years, I never tire of receiving comments. It's always a treat when someone emails me out of the blue and comments on how my post has affected them. I often think, *Wow, my words really did that for you?* Every one of us wants to feel a connection to others. The only way we can possibly know we have an effect on another is when we are told, so be sure to take the time and tell someone today how they have affected you.

♥ *Post inspirational messages on a billboard or create an inspiration jar.*

Thank a Company for Their Services

I ARRANGED AN appointment for a car service but had forgotten to record it in my calendar. When the car company called to remind me of my appointment, I realized that I would have missed it if they hadn't done so. Even though they'd just left a message, it was a personal message and not a recording, so I called back to say thank you and to tell them how grateful I was that they had just added this reminder call service.

• • • •

FOR AS LONG as I can remember, I have received reminder calls from doctor's offices, dentists, hairdressers, and other appointment-based businesses confirming scheduled appointments. It shouldn't surprise you that these reminder calls, while a wonderful nicety, are also crucial to their business. As a small entrepreneurial business owner for seven years, I learned the value of a reminder call myself. If you place a reminder call to a client, you improve the chances that someone will actually show up for an appointment. When I had the experience of a no-show, I could almost always pinpoint it back to the fact that I hadn't confirmed our appointment the day before. Whether we're talking about a business or personal appointment, receiving a reminder call from another human being is something to be grateful for—and it doesn't hurt to let those businesses know.

♥ *Call someone whose services you value and let them know why it is beneficial to you.*

CHAPTER 12

····

BLOW OUT
THE CANDLES

····

"The secret to staying young is to live honestly, eat slowly, and lie about your age."

—LUCILLE BALL

· birthdays ·

BIRTHDAYS ARE CELEBRATED differently all around the world. Although many cultures, like ours, celebrate with a party and cake, many cultures honor certain birthdays with particular rites of passage. In many Hispanic cultures, the Quinceañera marks the year a girl turns fifteen, while in Judaism, we celebrate a bar or bat mitzvah for our thirteen-year-old boys and twelve-year-old girls.

According to Jewish law, Jewish boys become bar mitzvah on their thirteenth birthdays, and Jewish girls become bat mitzvah on their twelfth birthdays. At this time, they are eligible to become full members of the Jewish community, assuming adult responsibilities for their choices and behaviors according to Jewish law.

Many bar and bat mitzvah students take on a mitzvah project as part of their celebration. These might include volunteering for an extended period of time for an organization like the Humane Society or Guide Dogs for the Blind; raising money for charitable organizations like the American Cancer Society or Magen David Adom; organizing a father-son charity baseball game; hosting a bike-a-thon or car wash; starting a food or toy collection drive; or even starting a nonprofit.

David Engle founded a nonprofit organization called Carnivals for Children on Wheels when he was just fourteen years old, as part of a bar mitzvah project. The idea is to bring free carnivals to children who are underprivileged and/or mentally or physically disabled.

Inspired several years ago as a bat mitzvah project by Julia Weiss, Oregon Jewish Community Youth Foundation (OJCYF) and its student board have since personally fundraised and allocated over $140,000 to over seventy nonprofits, primarily within the Portland, Oregon metropolitan area. In 2008, OJCYF was recognized by the Association of Fundraising Professionals Oregon and SW Washington Chapter as the Most Outstanding Innovative Philanthropy Project in Oregon.

ON THE OTHER side of the age spectrum are those Jews who celebrate a second bar mitzvah at age eighty-three. This has become increasingly more common as people are living longer. This custom follows the belief that the average life span is seventy years, so if you reach eighty-three, you are thirteen years into your second lifetime.

Any birthday is a time for celebration. I love the fact that the American Cancer Society (ACS) has become the sponsor for birthdays. Their mission is to help create a world with less cancer and more birthdays. Because a birthday symbolizes the completion of another year, the ACS reminds us how special one more candle, one more piece of cake, and one more celebration with the people we love really is. They have created an entire campaign to help more people celebrate more birthdays, and perhaps to give back as part of their celebration. My father only celebrated seventy birthdays. I think that was too few. I love this idea of utilizing a birthday as a celebration and as a way to give back.

In Judaism, as in other cultures, we also pay tribute on the anniversary of the death of our family members, leaders, and other loved ones. This custom allows for a different kind of celebration since the celebration of birth has less to do with the mark you've made on the world, or the people (other than your parents) you impacted during your life. John Lennon and I share the same birthday, and throughout my life I have met many Beatles fans who ask me if I know that I share his birthday. I have often wondered if these same folks would ask people born on December 8 if they knew they shared a birthday with the anniversary of John Lennon's death. A good friend of mine was born on November 22, 1963, the day President John F. Kennedy was shot. Her mom often shared with her that everyone in the hospital was bawling, except her because she was the proud and exuberant mother of a brand-new baby girl.

When I began the mitzvah project, it seemed like a relatively small thing to be taking on. Now that it has helped me move beyond grief to a place of inspiration and has informed a new chapter of my life, I hope that this 1,000 mitzvah project will be part of the legacy I leave for the world. I hope my own kids will celebrate the anniversary of my passing just as we've always celebrated birthdays—by honoring what really matters. In my life, I want to be able to say that I lived my life on purpose rather than that I lived a life just passing the time.

Help Celebrate a Missed Birthday

MY DAUGHTER'S NINTH birthday was a very special one for her. She invited three close friends for a sleepover at a local hotel. At the last minute, one of her friends got sick and had to miss the entire sleepover. She missed swimming in the pool, free snacks and drinks in the lobby, and the continental morning breakfast. The next day, my daughter wanted to bring her friend a piece of cake to help include her in the celebration. It turned out that her friend wasn't so much sick as she was nervous about sleeping away from her family. Bringing her some cake the next day turned out to be a great way to have her feel included in the event.

• • • •

WHEN MY KIDS were born, I told my husband I had no intention of throwing them giant birthday parties. I believed our kids didn't need this kind of fanfare to celebrate their birthdays, and that if we showered them with massive birthdays when they were little, they would have high expectations of what their birthdays were supposed to look like when they grew up.

I lucked out as a young mother because my daughter always wanted to have her birthdays at home. The majority of her twelve birthdays to date have been held in our home. When she was two, I took a cake-decorating class to make fancy-looking cakes, and I've made most of her cakes every year since.

It's been harder to have home parties with our son, whose birthday falls in the winter. The rainy Oregon days coupled with a tremendous amount of boy energy makes home birthdays less optimal for him. For several of his birthdays, we opted for more kid-themed location-based parties, but I have still limited the amount of children we invite.

. . . .

There is a huge disparity, not only among families in the United States, but also around the world, in terms of what birthday celebrations look like. Many children never have extravagant celebrations. There are plenty of ways for parents to utilize a birthday as a time to teach their children about appreciation. How about volunteering at a nonprofit or donating toys as part of your birthday celebration? You could have a party where you create blankets for a nonprofit like Binky Patrol, which makes sewn, knitted, crocheted, or quilted blankets to give to children at hospitals, emergency shelters, and other parenting projects.

A few years ago, I learned about an organization called Birthday Angels. This is a nonprofit located in Israel that partners with mentoring organizations that work with underprivileged children to help create birthday parties for Jewish, Bedouin, Arab, Russian, and Ethiopian children. In Israel, one in three children cannot afford a party. For a donation of $36, someone in the United States or the U.K. can sponsor a child's birthday, and the mentoring organization provides party kits full of games, decorations, music, and stickers—everything needed to help make a child's birthday into a celebration.

♥ *Donate to a charity that helps others celebrate their birthdays.*

Give or Do to Celebrate Your Birthday

FOR MY DAUGHTER'S ninth birthday, she told me she wanted me to ask her friends to give money to a charity in her honor instead of birthday presents. We had raised money and visited the Oregon Humane Society the previous summer, so this became her charity of choice. Two moms donated in her honor, and she received cards from the organization letting her know. In addition, she received some money that year and asked if we could buy flowers for an elderly friend of the family whom I was planning to visit that week.

. . . .

BIRTHDAYS ARE OPPORTUNITIES. Not only do they mark the passage of time, they're also chances for us to reflect on how we're living our lives and in what ways we might like to contribute to the world. Two years into the mitzvah project, I read a column in our local paper about Matt Strong, a young man who, at twenty-five, had already realized that things weren't going to make him happy. For his birthday, he asked his friends to do acts of kindness in his honor instead of giving him material gifts. He wanted them to send him an email to let him know what they had done. I was touched by his decision to forgo material birthday presents, and recognized in him a young man wise beyond his years.

Matt's idea inspired readers from the local community. One reader, Audeen Wagner, turned eighty years old on December 16, 2007, and she sent this note to her friends and family:

Dear Friends and Relatives,

I will be celebrating my eightieth birthday this December. Instead of buying a lovely and expensive gift for me, as I am sure you were planning to do, please do a good deed, then send me an email telling me what you did. It doesn't have to be a big deal, just an act of kindness...

In this world of distressing, depressing news—the war, the economy, politics, Mariners baseball—it is so refreshing to hear about seemingly small and insignificant acts that become a veritable landslide of loving concern for others.

Love, Grandma Audeen

Friends and family across Oregon, Washington, and California offered dozens of acts of kindness in her honor. People sent flowers, helped the homeless, gave to charity, volunteered in toy drives, and offered free babysitting. Many of Audeen's friends thanked her because her birthday request helped them get into action.

Perhaps instead of presents this year, you'll follow Matt and Audeen's lead. You never know whom you might inspire or motivate and how beneficial it will be for everyone involved!

♥ *Ask that others honor your birthday with acts of kindness instead of gifts.*

Surprise Someone by
Acknowledging Their Birthday

I DROPPED MY kids off at school one day, and learned that it was the birthday of a school mom I knew, whose family life was pretty complicated. When I went to the grocery store later that day, I bought some flowers to give her when I picked up my kids from school. The look on her face when I handed her the flowers and wished her a happy birthday was an incredibly rewarding experience.

• • • •

THIS MITZVAH REMINDED me of the MasterCard commercial that puts a price on a series of items and then lists one final thing that money can't buy and accompanies it with the voice-over that says, "Priceless."

The surprised look on this mom's face was priceless, and it made me happy to be the one who'd made her feel remembered.

I love being able to add the element of surprise to my life and others' lives. Birthdays are great for this. When we help someone else feel special, we are putting out positive energy, and in return we get more of it back.

I love when people go out of their way for me. A couple years ago on my birthday, an acquaintance called me to wish me a happy birthday. She didn't pretend like she knew all along; rather, she told me that she had been working on our networking group's newsletter that morning and writing up everyone's birthday for the month. When she got to my birthday and realized that it was that very day, she picked up the phone and called. I laughed out loud and told her that was the sort of crazy thing I would do, too, and I thanked her for making the call!

♥ *Go out of your way to wish someone happy birthday today.*

BLOW OUT THE CANDLES

Make a Cake

WHEN A CHEESECAKE Factory restaurant opened in our area, I couldn't wait to go out to dinner there. It's one of my favorite restaurants, and I'd long hoped they'd open a location in Portland. My family and I were just getting seated when we bumped into one of my daughter's elementary school teachers. She was out with a coworker and they were celebrating her birthday. Our family decided to surprise her with a piece of birthday cheesecake we had sent to her table. She loved this gesture, even though she told us the next day that she'd been too stuffed to eat it and had to take it home for later.

• • • •

DURING MY JUNIOR year in college in Los Angeles, my younger brother was working as a chef in Salt Lake City, Utah. I happened to mention on the phone a few weeks before my birthday how much I loved cheesecake. Unbeknownst to me, he went to work making me a cheesecake as a birthday gift, and he overnight FedExed it to me at school.

Unfortunately, the cake arrived on a Friday afternoon, a day when our college mail room closed earlier in observance of the Sabbath. No one contacted me from the mail room with my special delivery. On Monday morning, I learned about my priority mail, but I was heartbroken to see the beautiful homemade cheesecake covered with specks of blue mold. I never had the heart to tell my brother that all that hard work had spoiled over the weekend; nonetheless, it was one of the sweetest things someone has ever done for me on my birthday.

I know it sounds like a Hallmark card, but surprising someone with just the right gift says *I love you* like nothing else. Think about your friends and family throughout the year. If you create, find, or have something that's perfect for them, give it to them even if it isn't their birthday this month. Birthdays aren't the only reason to celebrate our lives!

♥ *Make or give something to someone this month even if it isn't their birthday.*

Send a Card to a Widower

WHEN MARCH ROLLED around again two years after my father died, his upcoming birthday made me think about what he and my stepmother would be doing on that day if he were still alive. I guessed they would be at a movie or show and definitely sharing a meal together. I wrote my stepmother a card to let her know I was thinking about her and called her on his birthday, too.

• • • •

THE HARDEST PART about losing someone is the ensuing days or years that still have special meanings, like birthdays and anniversaries, when that person isn't there anymore to share in your celebration and love. Even after someone has been gone for a few years, you still might wonder what they or you would have been doing with them if they were still alive. You imagine them a little older and you long to share some special things that are happening in your life, or you just miss them and wish you could hug and hold them.

When my dad was sick and dying, my husband told me about a Buddhist concept that says a person is like a firecracker. Their life sheds these bits of the fireworks everywhere, and after they're gone, there continues to be that small bit of each person inside of the people they touched during their lifetime. I know that I still carry a piece of my father with me.

♥ *Remember a friend or loved one even if it has been a while since they died.*

CHAPTER 13

····

DO UNTO OTHERS

····

*If you want happiness for an hour,
take a nap.
If you want happiness for a day,
go fishing.
If you want happiness for a year,
inherit a fortune.
If you want happiness for a lifetime,
help somebody.*

—CHINESE PROVERB

· *thought, speech, and action* ·

THE ENTIRE MITZVAH project can be summed up pretty simply in these few words: Sometimes you give and sometimes you receive. Being consciously aware that each and every day presents you with an opportunity to engage in positive ways with others only requires a subtle shift in perception. And acting on these small moments can and will affect your karma and the karma of the world at large.

Giving of yourself, your time, your energy, and your money is certainly gratifying for all the many ways we've discussed in previous chapters. But when you shift your entire way of being so that you are consciously in service to the world, you will see that more opportunities will come your way.

It also goes without saying that being the recipient of a mitzvah or an act of kindness can be a mood changer. Sometimes, by recognizing the power of giving, we ourselves become more in tune to all the small and subtle ways in which we also receive.

The mitzvahs themselves are generally very small actions we take toward helping or engaging others, and before I started my project, I didn't realize just how easy it is to go through our days without even noticing when someone is helping you. About six months into the mitzvah project, I discovered that I was often benefiting from observing others' mitzvahs. I realized that it was my general consciousness about mitzvahs that had changed.

I began watching people and noticing other people's mitzvahs, and in the process, I found that it opened up a well of positivity. In Judaism, there is a concept that one mitzvah begets another, or *mitzvah goreret mitzvah*. This comes from Pirkei Avot 4:2, also known as Ethics of our Fathers, when Rabbi Ben Azzai said: "Be eager to fulfill the smallest duty and flee from transgression; for one duty induces another and one transgression induces another transgression." The reward of a duty is a duty; the reward of one transgression is another transgression. When we do a good deed or when we witness someone else doing a good deed—like donating money or helping someone—it moves us to do the same again. This section is about noticing and observing. Sometimes we give and sometimes we receive, but until we can learn to receive, we can't adequately know what it is to give.

Visit a Friend in Need

JUST AFTER THE new year, I found out that a friend expecting her second child was on bed rest. I immediately empathized, since I'd been on bed rest with my son a few short years earlier. The entire month of November had passed by while I lay on the couch feeling physically healthy, yet bored and sad that I couldn't enjoy the beautiful crisp fall season happening right outside my front door. I remember negotiating with my unborn son, assuring him that I would stay still if he would keep growing and make it to full-term. I understood what my friend was going through, and I thought about all the things that I had appreciated during my month of bed rest. I picked up some sandwiches and kept her company while I folded some laundry and did a load of dishes.

• • • •

SOMETIMES WE JUST don't get it until we have been there ourselves. Personally, I find it hard to stand in someone else's shoes. Having gone through the loss of a parent has been a substantial lesson in grief, and it's an experience that has made me much more aware of how loss can affect others. In this case, having been on bed rest myself, I knew firsthand how hard it can be, and when I heard my friend was going through it, I knew I needed to act.

In the months after my father died, I taught a couple of classes with a local naturopathic doctor about moving from darkness to light. Some of the participants had lost loved ones, but others had lost a job or an animal. This was the first time I was among a group of people who had experienced great loss, and I felt I could truly relate to what they were feeling. I noticed how different it was to be with loss and grief having gone through it myself versus being with loss and grief before my father had passed. I felt more connected, and it made me realize the depth of understanding that comes through living something. If you're like me, you might have to go through something yourself before you can really get how it feels, but part of doing mitzvahs on a regular basis has to do with the practice of putting yourself in another's shoes. From there we access empathy, compassion, and understanding.

♥ *Whether you have a friend in the hospital, on bed rest, or who's just elderly and may need a helping hand, pay a visit and do some dishes or laundry.*

Accommodate Someone Else's Schedule

MY HUSBAND AND I were scheduled to attend our school's annual auction. Even though auctions aren't my husband's favorite type of event to attend, we'd decided to treat it as a date night, since dinner was included, and we were anticipating what interesting items we might bid on. About an hour before the event was supposed to start, our babysitter called to say that she had strep throat and couldn't babysit.

When we called our backup, not only did she agree to come over immediately, she canceled plans with her mom to do so. She arrived a half hour after we called her. Although we ended up being a little late to the event, we were thrilled to be a small part of the auction that raised $20,000 for our elementary school that evening.

• • • •

SOMETIMES WE NEED help in our lives. Whether it's something small or something big, it's important to acknowledge all the ways in which we work together to get where we need to be and do the things we commit to doing. Sometimes things don't work out, and in the scheme of things, not having a babysitter for an event you have planned to attend isn't a big deal. But when this babysitter went out of her way for us last-minute, it ended up having a ripple effect; it made us more grateful to attend an event that we had felt sort of ambivalent about before going. Sometimes it's the small gestures or efforts that change how we feel about humanity.

Every time I see this babysitter, even a couple years later, I still think about how she went out of her way for us. Each action we take in our lives has consequences. Maybe you want to be remembered as someone who goes out of their way and tries to help out when they can in whatever way they can. Nobody is perfect, of course, but action and effort go a long way. This mitzvah reminds me of a saying I love: Act as if what you do matters. It does!

♥ *Go out of your way to help someone, even if it might inconvenience you. It's good karma.*

Serve as the Go-Between

THE REBBETZIN CALLED me because she needed a Pack 'n Play for her granddaughter who was coming to town and bringing her small baby. We had given ours away years earlier, but I told her I would find one she could use. I placed a few phone calls and found a friend who was willing to lend hers out. I picked it up and brought it over to the rebbetzin's house.

• • • •

WHEN THE REBBETZIN called me, I could have just said, "We gave our Pack 'n Play away a long time ago," and left it at that. But I realized that I have access to more mothers than she does, and that it wouldn't take much effort to locate one so that she wouldn't have to keep looking.

Having your needs met in life is often about connecting with the right person or people. This is true in finding a job, meeting a mate, borrowing something, or coordinating an important event. When we connect with the right person, sometimes what feels difficult and trying on our end can be effortless because that person has the right connections or can just make things happen in ways we can't. In my case, I was the one who could make things happen with relatively little effort because I knew more young mothers than the rebbetzin. But I've been on the other side of this plenty of times in my life, too, and I've been so grateful for people who could easily figure out a solution to my problem and offered their help to do so.

Helping someone out, especially when it's a no-brainer and easy, is a fundamental mitzvah. Most people like to feel needed, so don't be afraid to connect with the right person for advice, help, or assistance.

♥ *Ask someone for help when you need it.*

Don't Hold a Grudge

ON A FRIDAY morning, I called a salon I had frequented for a few years to see if I could reschedule my appointment for another day. I had a cold and wasn't feeling well, but they informed me that they couldn't switch my time. When I showed up for my appointment, tissue box in hand, I must have been obviously annoyed when the owner came out ten minutes late for my appointment and proceeded to help someone else with no explanation to me. I grumbled to another client in the waiting room and to the receptionist. Later the owner came over and refused to serve me, and frankly I was quite taken aback. I didn't understand why she had acted this way with no explanation and was just irritated that I would have to forgo my appointment.

• • • •

DO NOT BEAR a Grudge is one of the 613 mitzvahs commanded of Jews. However, when this incident occurred, I was too irritated to consider the impact this interaction would have on me later. Instead, the first thought I had was to tell everyone about how disrespectfully I'd been treated at this salon. Many people want to retaliate when they are angry, and in that moment I felt the same way. In the end, however, I only shared the experience with my husband and decided that I wouldn't return to this salon anymore.

About two weeks later, although no longer so hot under the collar, I was still frustrated and upset by the situation. This is when it occurred to me that I was holding a grudge, and it was eating away at me since I couldn't let it go. I decided to call the owner to talk about it. I was so glad I did because talking it through allowed us both to see the misunderstanding between us. She thought I should have been more patient. I explained that I simply would have appreciated getting some notice or acknowledgment about the fact that there was a delay. We both forgave each other and I returned to her salon. Calling her and talking about it allowed me to return to the salon with the air cleared, and it also meant I could move forward in my day-to-day life without the burden of holding a grudge.

Even if it is easier to hold a grudge, asking for forgiveness lets you move forward and let go of that negative energy. During the Jewish holiday of Yom Kippur, Jews are required to ask forgiveness from those people whom we might have wronged. This could be a physical, emotional, or financial wrongdoing. We need to make an honest and heartfelt apology, and we can do so up to three times, after which time the person is expected to wholeheartedly forgive us provided the plea for forgiveness was sincere. After this time, our sins are forgiven. This opportunity allows us to begin each Jewish New Year asking forgiveness, forgiving others, and starting a new year bearing no grudges.

♥ *Don't hold a grudge. Speak to the person with whom you are angry, ask forgiveness, and move on.*

Act with Patience

AS IS OFTEN the case for busy moms, I had a small window of time to get a few errands done before picking up my children after school. One of the errands was returning a small kitchen appliance that we'd decided not to keep. It took forever because the sales clerk had difficulty matching up the return slip with the item I was returning. I felt harried and annoyed and was struggling with myself to remain calm, but I kept my mouth shut and let her do what she needed to do to make the return. At the end of the transaction, I thanked the women for her help, realizing that she was trying her best.

• • • •

THERE ARE MILLIONS of little annoying things that happen everyday. Things break, people run late, or people aren't doing something the way you would do it. But perhaps the perspective of seeing the glass half-full rather than half-empty is important in cases like these. When you are feeling impatient, take a moment to put your situation into perspective. Take a deep breath and realize that you can choose to respond. No one else has the power to decide that but you. Sure, you can blame others, get irritated, be annoyed, yell at the person helping you, or decide you are powerless over the situation—or you can choose to react with patience and calmness, in words and actions. I am not saying this is an easy thing to do, but self-awareness in these situations is the first step toward making choices that make you feel better about yourself and that don't end up ruining your day and the day of someone else who may just be trying their best.

If you have ever traveled to or lived in Israel, you are familiar with the concept of *savlanut*, or the Hebrew word for "patience." Israelis will use this phrase when something goes wrong. They will also use a physical gesture by putting their thumb and first two fingers together, point their fingers toward their chest, and move them back and forth saying, *"Savlanut."* To an Israeli, this idea reminds us to take a deep breath and relax, because some things are out of our control. This idea of *savlanut* helps Israelis not get frustrated when waiting in line endlessly, or dealing with the mundane frustrations in their lives. We can all use this concept of *savlanut* to remind ourselves that we don't have control over everything, and when we relinquish this control, it helps us maintain perspective in our lives.

♥ *Choose to remain calm in your words and actions.*

```
.................................
:    MITZVAH 554          :
.................................
```

Be a Mensch*

WHILE VISITING MY in-laws in Florida, I offered to help carry a frail
older gentleman's groceries into his apartment building. He told me he
didn't need my help, but thanked me for offering just the same. Then
he proceeded to tell me a story about another woman who had recently
helped him get his wife from her wheelchair into their car. He told me
that he greatly appreciated this woman's help, and was often surprised
but grateful when strangers took the time to offer him assistance. He
mentioned that it had gotten increasingly difficult for him to assist his
wife alone, so each stranger who helped him was a real mensch.

• • • •

LATER THAT DAY, my father-in-law ran into this neighbor, who mentioned how much he'd appreciated my offer to help. Sometimes our
assistance will be accepted and other times it won't be, but being a
mensch has a far-reaching impact.

When I think about the things I learned during this mitzvah project, one of the lasting lessons is that we are presented with the opportunity to help someone every single day. Whether or not we act on those
opportunities is completely up to us. I didn't set out to save the world. I
don't even profess that any of my 1,000 small actions stand out as particularly important or life-changing. But I will assert that each of them
made a small impact, and that cumulatively they have changed my life.
Every day, keep your eyes open for the little things you can do to help
another person. Start paying attention and become a mensch.

♥ *Stop and offer your assistance whenever you can.*

*Mensch, derived from Yiddish, is a person of integrity and honor.

Apologize for Your Actions

ONE NIGHT AFTER dinner, my husband and I decided we'd go to the gym and trade off kid duty. The plan was for my husband to leave first in his own car to get a head start on his routine and for the kids and me to meet up with him toward the end of his workout, after which I would attend a yoga class and he'd take the kids home. There would be a fifteen–minute window during which neither of us would be with our kids, ages ten and seven at the time, so we planned to let them sit together in the ladies' room lounge, which had a TV.

I got the kids settled and turned to go into the locker room to get ready for class, at which point I overheard an attendant tell my son he was too old to be in the women's lounge. I was rankled by the idea that he couldn't wait for me for those few minutes, and I was rude when I gave the attendant a piece of my mind.

I was so distracted during yoga thinking about how badly I had treated this attendant that I didn't have a good class. As soon as class ended, I found her and apologized. I told her I knew I had handled myself poorly and was embarrassed at my behavior. She forgave me and even offered to watch our son herself in the future if we ever found ourselves in a pinch with no acceptable place to leave him.

• • • •

LIKE ANYONE, I have my moments of being patient and impatient, but it's unlike me to hit the roof and lose my temper. In this instance, I was frustrated by the situation and took it out on the messenger who held fast to the rules of the gym. Luckily, I realized my mistake almost immediately and was able to rectify the situation quickly. It turned out to be a good lesson in many ways. Since I had acted inappropriately in front of my children before my class, I later told them that I had apologized for my rude behavior and that I'd been forgiven. My children and I had the opportunity to discuss together what asking for forgiveness does for both parties.

♥ *Apologize when you have misspoken to someone.*

Support a Cause

MOST SUPERMARKETS, PHARMACIES, and other stores do fund drives for community nonprofit organizations. Usually, when you donate, they'll put your name on a cutout and hang it somewhere in the store. On this particular day, I was at my local grocery store with my kids and saw they were doing a fund drive for the Muscular Dystrophy Association. I had given a dollar or two the last few times I'd stopped in, but this time the clerk explained to me that they had a store goal of $3,500 and that they had already raised over $2,200. If they hit their goal, they would help send four local kids to camp. She was so passionate when she described their goal that I gave again.

• • • •

THE FIRST TIME I'd given money for this cause, I hadn't thought about the local impact on our community, or the fact that the clerks had any investment in hitting a particular goal. When this clerk told me about the goal, however, her desire to reach it was so clear that I didn't even hesitate to give.

During this project, I donated to many causes when asked, including a Juvenile Diabetes Walk for friends whose son had recently been diagnosed, and for my young cousin in New York who emailed to see if I'd help her reach her goal of $1,800 for the Avon Breast Cancer Walk. I have spoken about this mitzvah before, but it's one that comes up so often that it's important to address. When someone reaches out to you and asks you to support an organization or a cause, consider the weight that it carries for them. It's oftentimes not easy for people to ask for money. You may find that people don't follow up with you to ask again. That doesn't mean that you're off the hook! It means that there's still an opportunity to give.

My husband's cousin was diagnosed with multiple sclerosis in her twenties. After her daughter took a teen tour to Israel in 2000 and climbed Masada, an important landmark in Israel, she promised herself she would someday hike Masada with her daughter. It was a fairly ambitious goal considering her health conditions, but she was determined. She decided she was also going to raise money for the MS society as part of her climb, and she started a website, www.howwilligetbackdown.com, which allowed people to learn about her story and donate to the charity. She raised more than $12,000 for the MS society, and we were thrilled to be able to share in her journey and contribute.

Each of us has causes and organizations we support with our time and dollars. Sometimes it can feel difficult because of the number of requests we receive, but I have rarely seen an organization be disappointed because I could only give five or ten dollars. In the case of my husband's cousin, most of that $12,000 came from sums ranging from eighteen to one hundred dollars, with a few larger ones thrown in. If you are worried that your small gift isn't enough, forget about it. Every gift counts, and it all adds up!

♥ *Support someone else's mission or cause.*

CHAPTER 14

····

OH, THE PLACES
WE'LL GO!

····

"If you reject the food, ignore the customs, fear the religion, and avoid the people, you might better stay home."

—JAMES MICHENER,
AMERICAN AUTHOR

· traveling and vacations ·

OUR NATIONAL WORK ethic is one of long hours and long weeks. Some people even pride themselves on never taking vacations. I am definitely not one of those people. I have been fortunate to travel to many countries and U.S. states in my lifetime, and I love being on vacation. It's always a thrill to travel to a new place and experience new cultures and environments.

When my brother and I were teenagers, we traveled, by car or in our family's camper, for most family vacations. Often we would go to New York City to visit our paternal grandmother. There were no videos or DVDs to keep us entertained during the drive. We played games, sang, and probably asked "Are we there yet?" enough times to drive my father and stepmother crazy.

During my junior year of high school, we took a family trip to England. My parents didn't book any hotels in advance, so each day, as we drove through the countryside of England, we started looking for a B&B once we started getting tired. It was such an adventure, and I remember thinking how carefree that trip felt. I have never taken a trip as loose and unstructured since, preferring to know where my family will stay each night on our family vacations. That said, I am still open to a loosely structured itinerary on vacation. Usually that means knowing what sights we must see and which ones are optional. Over the years, this flexible attitude has made for many wonderful spontaneous opportunities on vacation.

Many Jews say the traveler's prayer, or *Tefilat HaDerech*, when they travel by air, sea, or even on long car trips. It's a prayer asking for protection on the journey. I first learned about this prayer during a year abroad in Israel. I purchased a small card with the prayer printed on it before returning to the States. Nowadays, you can find the traveler's prayer on iPhone apps.

In addition, many Jews attend synagogue and receive the *Birkat HaGomel* blessing. This blessing thanks God for allowing a safe return. *Birkat HaGomel* is also said after surviving illness, childbirth, or any other near-death experience.

I mentioned in Chapter 5, "Dollars and Sense—Money," that there is another custom to give a friend or family member some *tzedakah* before they leave for a trip to donate once they've arrived safely at their destination (Mitzvah #550). An individual embarking on a trip with a mission to deliver *tzedakah* on the other end is somehow protected. It is thought that being the messenger of this *tzedakah* protects them in their travels.

We took a couple of trips while I was doing this project, and therefore most of the mitzvahs I detail here happen in Spain and Hawaii. I discovered we can be anywhere in the world and do mitzvahs, even if we don't speak the same language or have the same customs.

Share Your Umbrella

ON THE FIRST afternoon of our family vacation in Hawaii, I was lamenting the fact that we had to rent umbrellas on the beach. They were expensive, and my husband and I concluded that they weren't worth the price. A few minutes later, a man approached us to say he and his family were headed back to the mainland and offered to sell us his store-bought umbrella and chairs. He caught us off guard with his offer, and my husband and I said we needed a minute to discuss it. When I went back to accept his offer, he said he'd just decided to give them to us instead. We were thrilled to receive this gift, and I promised I would pay it forward, which we did on the last day of our trip when we passed them along to a nice family from New Jersey. It was wonderful to give and receive a mitzvah all in one.

• • • •

WE HAVE BEEN fortunate to travel to Hawaii several times because my mom and stepfather own a time-share property there. As on most vacations, there are items you decide to splurge for and others that you decide you can live without—like an umbrella at the beach.

On one of our first visits to Hawaii, my mom discovered that many guests leave items in the communal laundry room at the end of their trips. We have found toys and beach gear and even unopened food items left behind by guests. The local Goodwill is another great resource for vacation needs. We have found bats and balls, picnic goods, and other fun beach games that have made our vacations more fun and affordable.

Having vacationed at this property for so many years, we have befriended the concierge. One time he showed up with a boogie board for my son to use on the beach. For an eight-year-old, it was a wondrous gift, and probably not something we would have purchased for him ourselves.

At the end of a trip, pass on what you can. It's fun to give it directly to another person or family, but if you can't do that, see if the front desk or concierge will take your stuff and pass it along.

♥ *Give any vacation amenities you aren't taking home to another person or family.*

Say *Muchas Gracias*

MY HUSBAND WAS attending an international conference in Madrid, Spain, and we'd arranged for my in-laws to watch the kids so I could join him for a week. We both needed to renew our passports, and even though we sent them in twelve weeks before our trip, they had yet to arrive the week before we were supposed to leave. I was desperately calling the passport agency—to no avail. Finally, they told me if I contacted my senator's office, they would be able to help speed things along. I called our senator, Ron Wyden, and received the assistance of a wonderful woman who made sure things moved forward. My passport arrived two days later via FedEx. I sent a thank you postcard from Spain.

• • • •

TRAVEL OFTEN REQUIRES that we put our lives and faith in the hands of strangers. We take airplanes, trains, and taxis driven by people we entrust to get us safely to our destination. We eat food prepared by others, and almost all of our daily needs are left to be attended to by others. The creature comforts of home are not there when we travel, and part of the fun of the experience is adjusting to new experiences. Even though I have an entire chapter devoted to saying thank you, this mitzvah reminded me how important it is to say thank you when you're traveling abroad. When you are enjoying the new experiences, take a few moments to thank those around you.

Our trip to Spain wouldn't have happened without the help of the senator's aide, or an offer by my in-laws to watch our kids. Both deserved and received heartfelt thank-you letters for making our trip possible.

♥ *Thank those who helped you take or enjoy your vacation destination.*

Assistance Comes in Many Languages

ONE OF THE things I love to do when we are abroad is to visit the local supermarket. It is always interesting to see the variety of foods and the ways that food is presented in other cultures. On our trip to Spain, the supermarket had lots of kiosks selling local art and jewelry, as well as many interesting food items, including more kinds of olives than I even knew existed, spices, and *turrón*, a nougat confectionery well-loved in Spain. During our visit, I saw a mother, toddler twins in tow, struggling to get a cart. I gestured to her, not knowing how to tell her in Spanish that I wanted to help, and she smiled and nodded while we adjusted her children into the cart.

• • • •

I DIDN'T NEED to speak Spanish to know that I could offer assistance to another mother who had her hands full.

When my husband earned a sabbatical for the summer of 2001 from the high-tech company he was working for, we planned a four-week family trip to Holland. My mother-in-law joined us and helped us care for the children, who were four and fourteen months at the time. I remember arriving at the local supermarket on the second day of our trip. We were jet-lagged and exhausted, but knew we needed food in the house as soon as possible.

We arrived at the store, got a shopping basket, and proceeded to fill it like we would in the States—for an entire week for our family. What I didn't know at that time was that Holland had already adopted the idea of reusable bags and we didn't have any with us. Also, the supermarket didn't accept credit cards. And finally, and probably most important, European city folks don't shop for an entire week. They buy what they need for a day or so and make much more frequent visits to their local food shops.

OH, THE PLACES WE'LL GO!

During our large supermarket shopping, we hadn't really thought about how we were going to transport our cumbersome purchase home on our bicycles. Luckily, a market employee spoke English and explained to us about our shopping bag options and told us where an ATM was located just a few blocks away. After my husband left to get some money, another grocery employee helped me put several items back so we could transport our groceries home in one trip that day. I was grateful that even though we hadn't known the customs in Holland, we weren't made to feel embarrassed by the employees—perhaps just a bit uninformed. It was an eye-opening experience.

♥ *Offer your assistance to someone who may not know the norms in your town, city, or country.*

Befriend a Parent on an Airplane

I NOTICED A mom traveling with two small children on our ten-hour flight to Spain. I talked with her a couple of times while she bounced her littlest one on her hip up and down the aisles during the long flight. At one point, her kids were starting to lose it, and I offered her a couple of granola bars. The effects of the bars lasted less than five minutes, but I do think she appreciated the gesture. I know I would have.

• • • •

WE HAVE DONE our share of flying with small children. I am always prepared for the journey with snacks, books, crayons, Play-Doh, sticker books, and more packed into my carry-on luggage.

Even with lots of distractions, long flights with small children can be very exhausting. It is always a relief when you board a plane and instead of being confronted by passengers who roll their eyes at you, you find other adults who actually offer you their time and attention. I am always surprised and relieved to get a welcoming seatmate on an airplane. It's amazing how little it takes to captivate a child with a game of peek-a-boo, or simply engage them by smiling and cooing.

As my kids have gotten older, we have relished how much easier the traveling has become. Nowadays, they are old enough to carry their own carry-on bags and luggage through the airport. The diaper bags, stroller, and extra car seat are all gone, replaced now by a portable DVD player with some old *I Love Lucy* episodes that can keep them happy for several hours. In recent years, we have arrived from our cross-country journeys relaxed and calm and ready to begin our family vacation.

♥ *Put yourself in the shoes of the parents traveling with small children. Offer a hand, a toy, or just a friendly smile rather than rolling your eyes.*

OH, THE PLACES WE'LL GO!

Pick Up the Silverware

WHILE TRAVELING IN Spain, we ate at many restaurants where the food was exquisite, despite the fact that Spaniards eat at nine or ten at night, much later than we are used to. Even the language barrier, and the fact that menus didn't often offer an English translation, didn't hinder us too much. We were fairly successful using our guidebook and transliteration to point out what we wanted to eat. One night at dinner, as I was walking to the restroom, a waitress carrying several things in her hands dropped some silverware she was carrying. I quickly picked up what had fallen and handed it to her. She smiled appreciatively.

• • • •

EVEN THOUGH I have no idea how to say "fork" or "spoon" in Spanish, language isn't necessary when you are trying to help another person. Hand gestures, vocal inflection, or even just a smile can often make your point. In this instance, I didn't need any of those things. Simply picking up the dropped silverware and handing it to the waitress was enough.

While living in Israel, I struggled to communicate in Hebrew since I'd taken very few classes up to that point. One of the integral parts of the program I attended was participating in a volunteer project. I volunteered at an organization called *Yad LaKashish*, Lifeline for the Old, where I was assigned to assist a woman named Leah who had learning disabilities and other special needs. She and I took walks and did other small projects together. Even though her primary language was Hebrew and mine was English, and our communication was largely through hand gestures and other visual cues, we managed pretty well.

Later that same year, I was paired with a family for several months while we lived on a kibbutz. A kibbutz is a community settlement, usually agricultural, organized under collectivist principles. While the language made it harder for me to communicate in a deep way with my adopted family, we were able to share many moments together, and I certainly felt welcomed and accepted by them despite my limited Hebrew vocabulary.

♥ *Acts of kindness have no language barrier. Remember to perform them abroad.*

Hold the Umbrella

WHILE MY HUSBAND and I were sightseeing in Spain on a rainy after-noon, I saw a gentleman at one of the landmarks in the city who was trying to take a picture while juggling his camera and bags and holding his umbrella with his chin to keep himself dry. I walked over to him and motioned that I would hold the umbrella over his head while he snapped his photo. He nodded and smiled graciously and proceeded to take the photo.

• • • •

I HAVE SAID this before in earlier chapters: It's never the major things we do in life that matter. It's the simplest of generosities for another: holding the door, picking up something that has been dropped, offer-ing our time and energy for another human being in need, or simply holding someone's umbrella while they take a photo. Not a big deal in any sense, but still these gestures acknowledge that we see that another person needs something and we step up to offer it without a second thought—whether we speak their language or not.

On one family vacation, we arrived at the airport and were check-ing in at our gate. My kids were eleven and eight at the time. At the next counter, I overheard a young woman, probably in her mid-twenties, explaining that she had just lost her wallet. While she had her board-ing pass, she had no other identification or credit cards. She asked the agent if the fifteen dollars she owed for her one piece of luggage could be charged to a credit card on file. The agent called over a supervisor to assist in the situation.

My heart went out this woman. I could only imagine a day of travel-ing with no money in my pocket and no options for something to eat or drink. I guess that is the Jewish mother in me. Also, I wondered how they would clear her through security without an ID.

As we walked away from the counter, I approached her and handed her a ten-dollar bill. I told her I hoped it made her day easier. My daughter, who hadn't overheard the interaction, asked why I'd given this woman money. When I explained what I had witnessed, my daughter questioned how I knew she was legitimate. I explained that I didn't think anyone would try to make up that kind of a story at the airport these days in hopes that someone would overhear and give them a few bucks. When the woman passed us again on the way to security, she thanked me profusely.

♥ *Help someone in a bind.*

Donate Miniature Toiletries
to a Homeless Shelter

I'VE NEVER MET anyone who would deny having taken the miniature bathroom supplies from a hotel upon checkout. I happen to consider them one of the luxuries of staying in a hotel. On a recent trip, I collected several toiletries, and when I got home I donated them to a friend who runs a potluck in the park that serves the homeless in our community.

. . . .

MOST OF US gather up our little toiletry items and don't think twice about it. When I was a kid, my father and stepmother had an entire bathroom drawer filled with mini-soaps. We used those regularly for years in our home. You probably have toiletries from a trip you recently took. Next time you're at a hotel, or come across them in your house, consider donating those toiletries to homeless organizations that can pass them along to their clients. Sometimes doing mitzvahs is just thinking about what we have access to and realizing the profound help that something as simple as shampoo and soap can be to someone who doesn't have daily access to such things.

♥ *Donate your small travel toiletries to a homeless shelter.*

Tip the Housekeeper

I HAVE MADE it a habit to tip the housekeepers when we stay at a hotel. There are two main reasons why I do this. The first is that I feel fortunate to travel and want to show my gratitude to the men and women who take care of the hotels I frequent. The second and probably more compelling for me is that when I was in high school in Vermont, I worked for one of the local motels in our small ski resort town. I didn't receive many tips as a housekeeper during that time, but the few I did receive literally had me smiling all day. I was so happy and grateful to the guest who'd left me the money that I can still remember that feeling twenty-five years later.

• • • •

HAVING WORKED BOTH as a housekeeper in high school and as a waitress all through college, I can tell you firsthand that tips are treasured. Service-oriented professions don't pay very well, and yet the work can be hard and tiring. I always try to remember how lucky I am to be on vacation and staying in a hotel that has been cleaned and maintained by a large crew of employees. Keeping this in mind helps me stay mindful of ways I can say thank you and give gratitude for this opportunity. The next time you are on a trip, remember to leave a tip for the housekeeper and perhaps a thank-you message for helping make your stay pleasant.

♥ *Tip the housekeeper.*

CHAPTER 15

THE FINAL GOODBYE

"Death ends a life, not a relationship."

—JACK LEMMON

· death and grieving ·

T
HERE IS SO much ritual around life and death in Judaism. By
the time my father died, I had lived through life cycle events,
including my daughter's baby-naming, my son's *brit milah* (cir-
cumcision), my own bat mitzvah, and my marriage. But I was unaware—
and ultimately deeply grateful—for the wisdom and structure Jewish
mourning rituals provide the bereaved. What I ultimately learned is
that each of us will experience death in our own way and at our own
pace. I started this mitzvah project out of grief, and it took quite a while
to complete it. Someone else might be compelled to do something
entirely different in honor of their loved one, and others may simply
keep their memory alive. Regardless of how we cope, allowing ourselves time to be with our grief is imperative. The mourning rituals in
Judaism gave me that space and opportunity.

Many Jewish communities have a *chevra kadisha*, or a Jewish
burial society. These groups are made up largely of volunteers, men
and women, who are specially trained in the sacred rites of *taharah*,
or the washing of the body in preparation for a proper Jewish burial.
Traditionally, the deceased is not left alone until burial. During this
time, a *shomer* (watcher) reads psalms and recites prayers on behalf of
the dead. Several members of my father's Wednesday morning group
volunteered to participate in this mitzvah for him.

The Jewish custom is to be buried in a simple wooden casket, and
there is no open casket viewing. It is a great honor to the deceased and
their family to make a donation to a charity in lieu of flowers.

Another Jewish mourning practice is *k'riah*, or the rending of the
mourner's garment. Usually the mourner will rend a shirt or blouse.
This symbolizes the tearing of the heart the mourner feels at the time
of loss, and it's also a visible symbol to the community that someone
has experienced a loss in their life. This custom comes from the biblical

story, when Jacob learns of his son Joseph's supposed death (Bereshit, Vayeishev 37:34): *"Then Jacob rent his garments and placed sackcloth on his loins; he mourned for his son many days."* The rending usually takes place at the funeral. In modern times, people sometimes tear a black ribbon instead of ripping their actual clothing and then pin the ribbon to their shirt.

After the funeral service, mourners participate in the final burial of the deceased. They come forward after the casket is placed in the grave and help fill the gravesite with dirt. Customarily, the immediate family takes a shovel, pointing down instead of up, and uses it to throw dirt into the grave. This custom is thought to show that life as we know it has been turned upside down, or to show reluctance to participate. After the first mourner places dirt on the casket, they place the shovel back in the dirt for the next mourner to avoid passing along their grief, or they might pass it to others directly to show their respect for the difficulty of this shared experience. This last act of *kevod ha-met* (respect for the dead) is considered the ultimate mitzvah because the deceased can offer no repayment or gratitude for this kindness.

Another mourning ritual is the meal of consolation, or *seudat havra'ah*, which we discussed in Chapter 1. Mourners gather at the synagogue after they return from the cemetery and partake in the meal of recovery. In addition to bagels and bread, peeled hard-boiled eggs are customarily served. They symbolize the cycle of life, continuity, and the need to move on.

After the funeral, the mourner and their family return to their home and begin the period of *shiva*, the most intense period of mourning. *Shiva* means "seven," and this ritual is observed for seven days. During *shiva*, a mourner is not supposed to wash themselves or their clothing, cut their hair, work, or have sexual relations. Mourners remain in their homes and community members come to them, sitting with them and quietly lending an ear to let the mourner share, laugh, or cry. It is a mitzvah to visit a mourner during this time, and it is one of the most important acts a community member can do. During this visit, known as the *shiva call,* bringing food is also welcome.

When *shiva* ends, the mourner leaves home for a walk around the block, symbolically reentering the world and commencing the *shloshim* period, the thirty days after death. During this time, mourners return to their regular jobs, but it is still considered a heightened time of mourning.

The mourner's prayer, or *kaddish,* is traditionally recited at the funeral and then said every day for eleven months after the burial of one's parent. Prior to my father's death, we discussed the idea of my saying *kaddish* in his memory. The *kaddish* can only be said in the presence of a *minyan,* or a group of ten people. Though I wanted to say the *kaddish,* I was also concerned that it might not be feasible to commit to attending synagogue every day. My father and I had discussed the fact that he hadn't said *kaddish* for his own father, but he had for his mother.

For me, the recitation of the *kaddish* prayer was beneficial to my healing. Even some of the more difficult experiences surrounding it were profound. For instance, during the first month of saying *kaddish,* I stood up in the women's section of the orthodox synagogue I was attending to recite the prayer. Because no man stood to say *kaddish* that day, the *ba'al tefillah* (service leader), who hadn't seen me, just continued the service. A woman spoke up on my behalf, prompting the service leader to back up the service for my recitation of the mourner's prayer. Through sobs and tears, I stumbled through the prayer. Though my father's death was still palpable, and it was a bit uncomfortable to be singled out, it was an experience I have never forgotten.

Visit a Dying Friend

IN NOVEMBER 2007, almost a year after my father died, our beloved rabbi, Yonah Geller, took a fall. I had spent many hours with him during that year, and he was still in the ICU at a local hospital when I heard the news. The email from the synagogue asked that no visitors go to the hospital, but I did not heed this request. After all the years he'd been our rabbi and all those breakfasts we'd shared in his kitchen, I knew I had to pay him a visit. When he died the next day, I was profoundly grateful for my decision.

· · · ·

THE RABBI AND his wife were not only our clergy, they were also dear friends. Though there was a fifty-year age difference between us, my husband and I felt a kinship with the rabbi and rebbetzin from the first day we arrived in Portland nearly fourteen years earlier. They came to visit us in the hospital after each of our children were born and had joined us for many dinners over the years. They were Old World people, and yet they brought a modern sensibility to the messages they delivered to our congregation. At first, I was torn about whether or not it was appropriate to go to the hospital, especially in light of the email's specific instructions. Wouldn't everyone in our community feel a need to go visit him, having been personally affected by this special man? I wasn't immediate family and I wanted to respect their request, but I thought of the stories the rebbetzin had told me about the countless visits she had made to the hospital when members of the community were ill, and how she would bring baked goods, or sometimes substantially more.

On impulse, I decided I would bring a nosh and only stay for a moment. I whipped up some banana bread and prepared to go to the hospital that afternoon. When I arrived, the rebbetzin had stepped out for a few moments and only their son and daughter-in-law were in the room. They allowed me a moment alone to speak to the rabbi. A flood of emotions came over me as I spoke to him. I thanked him for the wonderful man he had been to our family and to me personally. I mentioned all the dinners he had shared with our family, as well as the advice and support he had given me. It was a short visit, but one of the most memorable of my life. When he passed the next day, I felt like I had had closure, and was overcome by the gift of having been able to say goodbye. I had learned so much in the year since my father had died. I was acutely aware that memories help you keep a person alive inside of you. I had completed my first five hundred mitzvahs when Rabbi Geller died, and I dedicated the next five hundred not only to my father, but also to the memory of Rabbi Yonah Geller. I hoped to influence others in the way that he had influenced me.

♥ *Visit a dying friend, tell them you love them, and tell them why.*

Visit a Mourner During *Shiva*

As I MENTIONED in the introduction to this chapter, visiting a *shiva* house and making a *minyan* is a mitzvah in Judaism. After our rabbi died, I went to his house several times during the week of *shiva*. My eleven months of saying the mourner's *kaddish* for my own father ended during this week. It was bittersweet for me to say my final mourner's *kaddish* while paying a visit to the *shiva* house for my rabbi.

• • • •

ONLY PARENTS, SIBLINGS, children, and spouses have an obligation to sit *shiva*. The *shiva* period has two important purposes: It honors the dead, and it allows mourners a chance to grieve. In our modern world, mourning is too often not even acknowledged. People are expected to get on with their life just like normal, but after experiencing a loss, life feels anything but normal. In the days after my father died, I wanted to create a cocoon around my family. I felt the physical need to be close to my children and husband, to hug them and comfort them, and in so doing feel comforted myself. The *shiva* period provided me an opportunity for this intense initial feeling of grief. It allowed me to be at home with the people I loved and to have others come visit me.

♥ *Visit with someone after they have lost a loved one. Bring them a meal.*

THE FINAL GOODBYE

Acknowledge Someone's Loss

A FRIEND OF ours lost her niece after a two-year battle with cancer. She was just nine years old, and she died from osteosarcoma, a form of pediatric cancer. I sent a condolence card and made a donation in her memory.

• • • •

OFTENTIMES AFTER TRAGEDY comes inspiration. My friend's parents, Sammy's grandparents, were devastated by the loss of their granddaughter and decided to do something that would honor her memory. They set into motion a nonprofit called Sammy Rides: Grandparents Riding for the Health of Grandchildren to raise money and awareness about pediatric cancer. The unforeseen benefit of this project was that it also kept them active and vital in the aftermath of such a tragic loss. Their first project included a team of five senior citizens, and a sixty-day, 2,400-mile bicycle ride across the southern United States from Arizona to Florida.

I have often said that out of grief may come inspiration. You never know what you might create after loss.

♥ *Send a card or make a donation in memory of someone's loved one.*

Attend a Funeral

DURING THIS PROJECT, our community lost another one of our spiritual leaders, Rabbi Aryeh Hirschfield. He passed away while scuba diving with his family in Mexico. He was just sixty-five years old. I'd only attended his synagogue once, so it wasn't the same experience for me as losing Rabbi Geller, but we have close friends who are lay leaders at his synagogue, and I felt the deeper communal loss over his passing. I didn't attend the funeral because I decided I didn't know him well enough to attend, but later in the afternoon on the day of his funeral I was upset with myself that I hadn't attended. I heard from friends that almost a thousand people were there. Don't let the degree of intimacy (or lack thereof) be a reason for not attending a service.

. . . .

FUNERALS ARE A strange ritual. They aren't like other celebrations that you anticipate and plan for months. They are often planned within a day or two and are generally inconvenient or difficult for out-of-town guests to attend. And yet, they are incredibly valuable. Coming together with others to mourn and share our loss is crucial. In Judaism, all of the focus leading up to the funeral is on the deceased. They are washed and dressed and then watched and lovingly buried. Then, as soon as the funeral is over, the attention switches from the deceased to the bereaved. At my father's funeral, a synagogue full of people showed up. I knew some of them personally, but there were many I didn't know. As I looked around, I was moved by all of the people who had come to say goodbye. There is a closure that comes when you attend a funeral, and it is valuable for the healing that begins afterward. When I was in college, a very close childhood friend of mine died. We were only in our early twenties, and I was attending college in Los Angeles and couldn't afford to fly back to the East Coast to attend the funeral. Attending a person's funeral is a sign of respect, and it's a way to show solidarity with the grieving family, friends, and community.

♥ *Attend a funeral for a community member.*

Attend a *Yizkor* Service

I ATTENDED SYNAGOGUE during the last day of Passover, where it is the practice to commemorate a loved one during the *Yizkor* memorial service. This service is held four times a year—on Passover, Yom Kippur, and the last day of the Jewish holidays of Sukkot and Shavuot. These Jewish holidays are times to be with family, so they're perfect opportunities to remember family members who are no longer with us.

One of the key components of the prayer is a private pledge to give charity and do acts of kindness in honor of the deceased. Since I had never participated in the *Yizkor* service prior to my father's death, I was unfamiliar with the liturgy. My first reading of the English translation of the *Yizkor* service reaffirmed for me that I was on the right path with the mitzvah project. It reads: "In tribute to his memory I pledge to perform acts of charity and goodness."

• • • •

THE *YIZKOR* SERVICE is a very emotional service for many. It's a time to remember a loved one, maybe even to be in quiet conversation to tell them what is going on in your life, what you miss about them, what you are still angry about. It's a cleansing time, and for me it was a huge comfort in the aftermath of my loss. Sometimes you will not feel sad during these services, and that's okay. This day at synagogue I actually felt content. As I made my silent prayers and thought about my father, I felt at peace. I had learned so much since his death, and while I missed his physical presence, I had felt his spiritual presence many times. As the service ended, tears started welling up as I thought about many of my friends who hadn't yet experienced the loss of a parent. When I thought about what they still had to go through, I suddenly felt myself getting overwhelmed with emotion. I was sobbing and was completely surprised by what had triggered it. After the services ended, a friend asked if I was okay. I assured her that I was fine, but had lousy timing. But sadness and grief don't often have good timing. It's okay. Let it happen anyway.

♥ *Attend* Yizkor *services.*

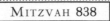

Light a *Yartzeit* Candle

IN JUDAISM, WHEN someone dies, we commemorate the anniversary of the deceased relative's death based on the Hebrew calendar. Because it's a lunar calendar, it changes from year to year, and this anniversary is called a *yartzeit*. It is customary to light a candle that burns for twenty-four hours. On the first anniversary of my father's death, I observed the day by going to synagogue. I was called up during the service and a special blessing was recited in memory of my father. The blessing talked about the deceased having been an inspiration, and it also urged doing charity in the memory of the deceased. I smiled knowing that I was already honoring my father through my mitzvah project.

• • • •

BEFORE MY FATHER died, we talked about how we might stay connected after he was gone. I told him I would be open to the signs. I remember saying, "If you come back as an animal, I will pay attention."

At his funeral, a black bird hovered at the top of the synagogue chapel. I saw it several times and decided that he had chosen that black bird as a sign to me. A few weeks later, I saw a black crow flying down the highway, keeping pace with my blue minivan. I looked over and could practically see the bird's eyes as it flew parallel to my car. It brought a smile to my face.

Over the next several months, I met the black crow a few more times. Once, I saw a group of crows outside of a local swimming pool where I exercise. It was 6 AM, a magical time of day. My father loved the early mornings, and I knew how much he appreciated the beauty of nature. I decided that the group of black crows was a signal from my father, the ever-social being. For me, they symbolized the new friends he had met on the other side.

I have certainly wondered over the years if it was just reassuring for me to think that the crows were a sign from my father. After all, it's a very common bird. But in the end it doesn't matter, because I have felt comforted by these experiences. It feels as if he's not so far away, and it's given me a tangible link and a way to continue a bond with my father that transcends our previous relationship. It has been a comfort and a beneficial part of my healing, and for that I am grateful.

♥ *Light a yartzeit candle, or another kind of candle, and say a prayer for your loved one on the anniversary of their death.*

Resources

Jewish Nonfiction Books

Artson, Bradley Shavit, *It's a Mitzvah: Step-by-Step to Jewish Living* (New York: Behrman House, 1995).

Chofetz Chayim, *Concise Book of Mitzvoth* (Jerusalem: Feldheim Publishers, 1990).

Dorff, Elliot N., *The Way into Tikkun Olam: Repairing the World* (Woodstock, Vermont: Jewish Lights Publishing, 2005).

Fuchs-Kreimer, Nancy, *Parenting as a Spiritual Journey: Deepening Ordinary and Extraordinary Events into Sacred Occasions* (Woodstock, Vermont: Jewish Lights Publishing, 1996).

Halberstam, Yitta, and Judith Leventhal, *Small Miracles: Heart-Warming Gifts of Extraordinary Coincidences* (Massachusetts: Adams-Media Corporation, 1998).

Kimmel, Eric, *Hershel and the Hanukkah Goblins* (New York: Holiday House, 1994).

Kimmel, Eric, *The Magic Dreidels* (New York: Holiday House, 1997).

Kushner, Harold S., *To Life: A Celebration of Jewish Being and Thinking* (New York: Warner Books, 1993).

Milgram, Goldie, *Meaning & Mitzvah: Daily Practices for Reclaiming Judaism through Prayer, God, Torah, Hebrew, Mitzvot and Peoplehood* (Woodstock, Vermont: Jewish Lights Publishing, 2005).

Salkin, Jeffrey K., *Putting God on the Guest List: How to Reclaim the Spiritual Meaning of Your Child's Bar or Bat Mitzvah*, third edition (Woodstock, Vermont: Jewish Lights Publishing, 2005).

Telushkin, Joseph, *Jewish Literacy: The Most Important Things to Know about the Jewish Religion, Its People, and Its History* (New York: Harper Collins, 2001).

Nonfiction Books on Death or Mourning

Berman, Rochel U., *Dignity Beyond Death: The Jewish Preparation for Burial* (New York: Urim Publications, 2005).

Brener, Anne, *Mourning & Mitzvah: A Guided Journal for Walking the Mourner's Path Through Grief to Healing*, second edition (Woodstock, Vermont: Jewish Lights Publishing, 2001).

Broner, E. M., *Mornings and Mourning: A Kaddish Journal* (San Fransisco, California: Harper Collins, 1998).

Coryell, Deborah Morris, *Good Grief: Healing through the Shadow of Loss*, third edition (Rochester, Vermont: Healing Arts Press, 2007).

Diamant, Anita, *Kaddish: How to Comfort the Dying, Bury the Dead, and Mourn as a Jew* (New York: Schocken Books, 1998).

Kübler-Ross, Elisabeth, *On Death and Dying* (New York: MacMillan Publishing, 1969).

Kushner, Harold, *When Bad Things Happen to Good People* (New York: Avon, 1997).

Lamm, Maurice, *The Jewish Way in Death and Dying* (New York: Jonathan David, 2000).

Levy, Alexander, *The Orphaned Adult: Understanding and Coping with Grief and Change after the Death of Our Parents* (New York: Perseus Publishing, 1999).

McCracken, Anne, and Mary Semel, *A Broken Heart Still Beats: After Your Child Dies* (Center City, Minnesota: Hazelden, 1998).

Welshons, John E., and Wayne W. Dyer, *Awakening from Grief: Finding the Way Back to Joy* (Makawao, Hawaii: Inner Ocean Publishing, 2003).

Wolfson, Ron, *A Time to Mourn, A Time to Comfort: A Guide to Jewish Bereavement*, second edition (Woodstock, Vermont: Jewish Lights Publishing, 2005).

Nonfiction Books Related to Kindness and Happiness

Conari Press, *Random Acts of Kindness* (San Francisco, California: Conari Press, 2002).

Post, Stephen, Ph.D., and Jill Neimark, *Why Good Things Happen to Good People: How to Live a Longer, Healthier, Happier Life by the Simple Act of Giving* (New York: Broadway Books, 2007).

Rubin, Gretchen, *The Happiness Project: Or, Why I Spent a Year Trying to Sing in the Morning, Clean My Closets, Fight Right, Read Aristotle, and Generally Have More Fun* (New York: Harper Collins, 2009).

Nonfiction Books Related to Life and Death

Albom, Mitch, *Tuesdays with Morrie* (New York: Doubleday, 1997).

Allende, Isabel, *Paula: A Memoir* (New York: Harper Collins, 1994).

Dann, Patty, *The Goldfish Went on Vacation: A Memoir of Loss (and Learning to Tell the Truth about It)* (Boston: Trumpeter Books, 2007).

Didion, Joan, *The Year of Magical Thinking* (New York: Alfred Knopf, 2005).

Izzy, Joel ben, *The Beggar King and the Secret of Happiness* (Chapel Hill, North Carolina: Algonquin Books, 2003).

Frankl, Viktor, *Man's Search for Meaning* (Boston: Beacon Books, 1959).

Goldman, Ari L., *Living a Year of Kaddish: A Memoir* (New York: Schocken Books, 2003).

Remen, Rachel Naomi, MD, *My Grandfather's Blessings: Stories of Strength, Refuge, and Belonging* (San Francisco, California: Berkley Publishing Group, 2000).

Books on Tzedakah

Salamon, Julie, *Rambam Ladder: A Meditation on Generosity and Why It Is Necessary to Give* (New York: Workman, 2003).

Siegel, Danny and Naomi Eisenberger, *Mitzvah Magic: What Kids Can Do to Change the World* (Minneapolis, Minnesota: Kar-Ben Publishing, 2002). Other book titles by Danny Siegel: *Giving Your Money Away: How Much, How To, Why, Where, and To Whom,* and *Gym Shoes and Irises (Personal Tzedakah).*

Judaism Online

My Jewish Learning: www.myjewishlearning.com

Judaism 101: www.jewfaq.org

Chabad: www.chabad.org

Jewish ritual: www.ritualwell.org

LIST OF CHARITIES

EVERY DONOR WANTS to make an informed decision where to give their money, and sometimes that can be a difficult choice. There are so many wonderful charities in the world, so the choice can be daunting. Before deciding where to give, think about what matters most to you. What geographic area and issues are near and dear to your heart? This will help you limit your scope somewhat.

A few online resources exist that might help you as well. Charitynavigator.org offers free online evaluations for more than 5,500 of America's largest charities. Guidestar.org is another online resource whose mission is to provide information that advances transparency, to enable users to make better decisions, and to encourage charitable giving. Please note that many smaller organizations won't be found on either of these lists. For smaller nonprofits, you may want to look at the mission statement of the organization. It should give you a clear understanding of why the organization was founded and what it intends to accomplish. Even small charities should be able to furnish you with their financial records if you'd like that to make your decision to give.

In this section, I have chosen to include charities I knew personally or that were recommended to me by reliable sources and were ones that I donated time or money to during the mitzvah project. I used the websites listed above for evaluation and inclusion in this section of ones that didn't meet that initial criteria.

Food-Related Organizations (In and beyond Portland, Oregon)

Challah for Hunger | *www.challahforhunger.com* | Challah for Hunger is a grass-roots nonprofit started by college students that raises money and awareness for hunger and disaster relief, through the production and sale of *challah* bread.

Feeding America | *800/771-2303* | *www.feedingamerica.org* | Feeding America, formerly America's Second Harvest, is the nation's leading domestic hunger-relief charity. Their network of more than 200 food banks serves all fifty states, the District of Columbia, and Puerto Rico.

Fork It Over! Metro | *503/797-1700* | *www.metro-region.org* | Portland Metro's food donation program to reduce hunger and waste in the Portland, Oregon metropolitan area.

Mazon | *310/442-0020* | *www.mazon.org* | *MAZON*: A Jewish Response to Hunger is a national, nonprofit agency that allocates donations from the Jewish community to prevent and alleviate hunger among people of all faiths and backgrounds.

Meal Train | *www.mealtrain.com* | Online resource to help communities organize meals for someone after any life cycle event. Effective and simple to use.

Oregon Food Bank | *503/282-0555* | *www.oregonfoodbank.org* | Distributes food to agencies that feed people who are hungry throughout Oregon and Clark County, Washington. Working to address the root causes of hunger through public policy and education programs.

Share Our Strength | *800/969-4767* | *www.strength.org* | This national nonprofit raises money to support the local organizations serving American children the food and nutrition they require.

Sunshine Pantry | *971/506-7827* | *www.sunshinepantry.org* | Sunshine Pantry is a nonprofit pantry offering food, clothing, household items, toys, and toiletries to families in need in Beaverton, Oregon.

Social Action Organizations

American Jewish World Service | *800/889-7146* | *www.ajws.org* | A nonprofit organization dedicated to providing nonsectarian humanitarian assistance and emergency relief to disadvantaged people worldwide.

Change.org | *www.change.org* | Change.org raises awareness about important causes and empowers people to take action with leading nonprofits.

Do Something.org | *212/254-2390* | *www.dosomething.org* | Using the power of *online* to get teens to do good stuff *offline*.

HandsOn Network | *404/979-2900* | *www.handsonnetwork.org* | HandsOn Network inspires, equips, and mobilizes people to change lives through service. This organization has a plethora of information and can help you find volunteer opportunities in your community.

Points of Light Institute | *404/979-2900* | *www.pointsoflight.org* | Points of Light Institute inspires, equips, and mobilizes people to take action that changes the world. The Institute has a global focus to redefine volunteerism and civic engagement for the twenty-first century, putting people at the center of community problem-solving.

Organizations Helping Children or Families

Areyvut | *201/244-6702* | *www.areyvut.org* | Enables Jewish youth to infuse their lives with the core Jewish values of *chesed* (kindness), *tzedakah* (charity), and *tikkun olam* (social justice).

Big Brothers Big Sisters | *215/567-7000* | *www.bbbs.org* | National youth-mentoring organization. Helping children realize their potential and build their future.

Binky Patrol | *www.binkypatrol.org* | All-volunteer, nonprofit organization dedicated to making blankets and giving them away to children who are ill, abused, or in shelters or hospitals.

Boys and Girls Club | *800/854-CLUB* | *www.bgca.org* | Increasing numbers of boys and girls are at home alone in communities all over the country. Boys and Girls Clubs offer programs and services to promote and enhance the development of boys and girls by instilling a sense of competence, usefulness, belonging, and influence.

Carnival for Kids on Wheels | *www.cfcow.org* | In 2007, the summer before he went into ninth grade, David Engle created Carnivals for Children on Wheels to bring carnivals to children who are underprivileged or mentally and/or physically disabled. After just three years, David has built a volunteer crew and has personally volunteered close to 500 hours to bring these carnivals to the children.

Friendship Circle | *248/788-7878* |*www.friendshipcircle.org* | Friendship Circle provides assistance and support to families of children with special needs. Started in Metro Detroit, with most of the innovative work with special-needs children happening at the Ferber Kaufman LifeTown Building, Friendship Circles now exist in over eighty locations in twenty-two states and seven countries.

Junior Achievement | *719/540-8000* | *www.ja.org* | International nonprofit teaching youth about work readiness, entrepreneurship, and financial literacy through experiential programs.

Sammy Rides | *www.sammyrides.com* | Grandparents Riding for the Health of Grandchildren, raising money for Pediatric Cancer Research.

Soles4Souls | *866/521-SHOE* | *www.soles4souls.org* | Soles4Souls is a shoe charity that donates shoes to adults and children in need. Contact them to donate shoes, host a shoe drive, or help provide disaster relief.

Sports Gift | *949/388-2359* | *www.sportsgift.org* | Nonprofit focused on providing sports to underprivileged children throughout the world and promoting sports-related community service among our youth. Their work improves the lives of and gives hope to impoverished children through a variety of sports programs.

Youth Philanthropy

National Youth Leadership Council | *651/631-3672* | *www.nylc.org* | For more than two decades, NYLC has led a movement empowering youth to transform themselves from recipients of information and resources into valuable, contributing members of a democracy. Find links to programs, services, and new stories on their website.

Oregon Jewish Community Youth Foundation (OCJYF) | 503/248-9328 | www.orjcf.org | An initiative of OCJF designed to fuel a lifelong passion for philanthropy and social action. Through OJCYF, students develop an understanding on nonprofits and their inner workings. Serves youth in the Portland metropolitan area.

Youth Service America | *202/296-2992* | *www.ysa.org* | Youth Service America (YSA) is an alliance of 300+ organizations committed to increasing the quantity and quality of service opportunities for young people. Their goal is to educate youth, teachers, community organizations, media, and public officials in the power of youth as problem solvers and to engage children and youth as volunteers, as academic achievers, and as community leaders.

What Kids Can Do (WKCD) | *401/247-7665* | *www.whatkidscando.org* | National nonprofit founded in January 2001 by an educator and a journalist who support adolescent learning in and out of school. Organization works to promote perception of young people as valued resources, not problems, and to advocate for learning that engages students as knowledge creators and not simply test takers.

Organizations Promoting Self-Sufficiency

Dining for Women | *864/335 8401* | *www.diningforwomen.org* | Dining for Women's mission is to empower women and girls living in extreme poverty. This organization funds programs that foster good health, education, and economic self-sufficiency and cultivates educational giving circles that inspire individuals to make a positive difference through the power of collective giving.

Dress for Success | *212/532-1922* | *www.dressforsuccess.org* | International nonprofit organization that provides interview suits, confidence boosts, and career development to low-income women worldwide.

Goodwill Industries International | *800/741-0186* | *www.goodwill.org* | Goodwill is not only a location for donating your usable goods, it is also an international organization committed to offering work opportunities that enhance the lives of individuals, families, and communities. Their mission is to help people reach their fullest potential.

Habitat for Humanity | *800/422-4828* | *www.habitat.org* | A nonprofit, ecumenical Christian housing organization building simple, decent, affordable housing in partnership with people in need.

Heifer International | *888/422-1161* | *www.heifer.org* | Nonprofit organization whose goal is to help end world hunger and poverty through self-reliance and sustainability.

Itafari | *503/954 1096* | *www.itafari.com* | Grassroots efforts to help the women of Rwanda rebuild their nation.

Salvation Army | *800/728-7825* |*www.salvationarmyusa.org* | The Salvation Army is another well-known place to donate usable clothing, furniture, or other household items. They also take donations of airline miles, automobiles, and money. The Salvation Army is committed to building communities through disaster-relief efforts, youth and senior programming, and their community care ministries.

Unicef—United States Fund | *800/367-5437* | *www.unicefusa.org* | Working in over 150 countries, UNICEF is a global humanitarian relief organization providing children with clean water, nutrition, education, emergency relief, and health care. The U.S. Fund for UNICEF supports their humanitarian relief work through fundraising, advocacy, and education in the United States.

United Way | *703/836-7112* | *www.unitedway.org* | United Way Worldwide is a nonprofit organization providing leadership and services to a network of member United Way communities, donors, and partner organizations across the world.

Israeli-Based or Related Organizations

American Friends of Magen David Adom (AFMDA) | *866/632-2763* | *www .afmda.org* | Magen David Adom and its team of trained volunteer and professional medical responders depend on AFMDA support to provide the entire Israeli nation with pre-hospital emergency needs, including medical, disaster, ambulance, and blood services.

Big Brothers Big Sisters of Israel | *www.bigbrothers.org.il* | The oldest, largest, and most effective youth mentoring organization in the world. Big Brothers Big Sisters of Israel recruits and supports long-term mentors who meet weekly with children, ages five through eighteen, from isolated single-parent homes.

Birthday Angels | *www.birthday-angels.org* | Nonprofit organization that helps provide every child in Israel with his or her own birthday party. In 2006–2009, over 7,000 underprivileged children celebrated their birthdays thanks to the Birthday Angels volunteers and generous donations.

Hadassah | 888/ 303-3640 | *www.hadassah.org* | A women's volunteer Zionist organization, whose members are motivated and inspired to strengthen their partnership with Israel and ensure Jewish continuity.

Humans and Animals in Mutual Assistance (HAMA) | c/o Jewish Causes of Choice | *781/433-9080* | *www.jchoice.org* | HAMA is an animal therapy organization based in Israel. It helps a wide range of people, including terror victims, the mentally challenged, Holocaust schizophrenics, and victims of domestic abuse. These people have failed traditional methods of intervention, and animal therapy affords them a unique opportunity to regain psychological health.

Jewish Causes of Choice | *781/433-9080* | *www.jchoice.org* | An online resource for traditional Jewish giving. Makes it very simple to give and provides a forum for teens to dialog with their peers and the programs themselves, directly learning the impact of their donations.

Mitzvah Heros Fund, Inc. | *301/335-6278* | *www.mitzvahheroesfund.org* | Founded by students of Danny Siegel after his nonprofit Ziv Tzedakah (*www .ziv.org*) was formally closed. This nonprofit collects and distributes funds to deserving little-known *tzedakah* projects. Their primary interest is seeking out mitzvah heroes, good people making things happen, with a minimum of operational procedures and bureaucracy and a record of exceptional fiscal responsibility. They believe that money can be used to make miracles happen: It can change people's lives for the better; restore dignity; provide jobs, food, freedom, and well-being for desperate people; and, most of all, offer hope.

Rabbanit Bracha Kapach | c/o Jewish Causes of Choice | *781/433-9080* | *www .jchoice.org* | The rabbanit's nonprofit is called Keren Segulat Naomi in memory of her mother. For more than forty-five years, Rabbanit Bracha Kapach has distributed food to people in need including *challahs*, chicken, and other basic items for Shabbat. She also distributes thousands of Passover packages with a huge volunteer staff.

United Jewish Communities (UJC) | *212/284.6500* | *www.jewishfederations.org* | The Jewish Federations represents 157 Jewish federations and 400 network communities, and it raises and distributes more than $3 billion annually for social welfare, social services, and educational needs. The Federation movement protects and enhances the well-being of Jews worldwide through the values of *tikkun olam* (repairing the world), *tzedakah* (charity and social justice), and *Torah* (Jewish learning).

Health-Related Organizations

American Heart Association: Jump Rope for Heart | *800/AHA USA 1* | *www.americanheart.org* | Nonprofit whose mission it is to build healthier lives, free of cardiovascular diseases and stroke.

American Cancer Society | *800/227-2345* | *www.cancer.org* | International nonprofit dedicated to helping people who face cancer. Supports research, patient services, early detection, treatment, and education.

American Red Cross | *202/303-5000* | *www.redcross.org* | The nation's premier emergency response organization. Today, in addition to domestic disaster relief, they offer services in five other areas: community services that help the needy; support and comfort for military members and their families; the collection, processing, and distribution of lifesaving blood and blood products; educational programs that promote health and safety; and international relief and development programs.

Doctors Without Borders | *212/679-6800* |*www.doctorswithoutborders.org* | Doctors and nurses volunteer to provide urgent medical care in countries to victims of war and disaster regardless of race, religion, or politics.

Leukemia & Lymphoma Society: Pennies for Patients | *800/955-4572* | *www .leukemia-lymphoma.org* | National nonprofit dedicated to curing leukemia, lymphoma, and myeloma, and to improving the quality of life of patients and their families.

Muscular Dystrophy Association | *888/435-7632* | *www.mda.org* | Nonprofit that provides services and resources to families affected by neuromuscular disorders.

Make-a-Wish Foundation | *800/722-9474* | *www.wish.org* | Nation's largest wish-granting organization. The Make-A-Wish Foundation gives hope, strength, and joy to children with life-threatening medical conditions.

St. Jude's Research Hospital | *901/595-3300* | *www.stjude.org* | America's third largest health-care charity, pioneering procedures to help seriously ill children.

Environmental Resources

The Baltimore Free Store | *410/340-9004* | *www.thefreestorebaltimore.org* | We've been told "bigger, better, more" is the way to live, but that is simply not true. If you live in the Baltimore metropolitan area, free yourself from the burden of *stuff*. BFS accepts donated or salvaged goods and redistributes them at their store in Baltimore City at no charge.

ChicoBags | *888/496-6166* | *www.chicobag.com* | Specializes in offering compact reusable bags and lifestyle totes that are fashionable, environmentally friendly, and designed to be unforgettable.

Community Resource Warehouse | *503/235-8786* | *www.communitywarehouse .org* | Community Warehouse is a nonprofit that recycles donated furniture and household items by giving them to individuals and families recovering from crisis. Serves the greater Portland, Oregon metropolitan region.

Earth 911.com | *800/CLEANUP* | *www.earth911.com* | An environmental website that provides the information and tools you need to live a greener lifestyle and make every day Earth Day. Site includes links to recycling centers, how to recycle, pollution prevention, and how to help protect the environment.

Free Change | *www.free-change.org* | Free Stores are locations where food, household necessities, and services are made available to visitors at no cost. Everything that is available at the Free Store is donated, and the operation is facilitated by volunteers. This store, located in SE Michigan, serves a broad range of clients.

Jewish National Fund | *888/JNF-0099* | *www.jnf.org* | Plant Trees In Israel. Nonprofit organization specializing in development of Israeli land and infrastructure, especially planting trees.

National Audubon Society | *212/979-3000* | *www.audubon.org* | The mission of the National Audubon Society is to conserve and restore natural ecosystems, focusing on birds and other wildlife for the benefit of humanity and the earth's biological diversity.

The Nature Conservancy | *800/628-6860* | *www.nature.org* | The Nature Conservancy protects Earth's most important natural places for you and future generations through great science and smart partnerships.

SCRAP—School and Community Reuse Action Project | *503/294-0769* | *www.scrapaction.org* | Nonprofit that works to inspire creative reuse and environmentally sustainable behavior by providing educational programs and affordable materials to the Portland, Oregon metropolitan community.

Terracycle | *609/393-4252* | *www.terracycle.net* | Private company that specializes in up-cycling, creating a range of consumer products from post-consumer materials. Terracycle offers Brigades, or national programs where nonprofits or schools can earn cash for their trash.

Washed Ashore | *541/347-2859* | *www.washedashore.org* | The Washed Ashore project is sponsored by the nonprofit Artula Institute for Arts and Environmental Education. Their mission is to provide opportunities to express and teach environmental issues through the arts. Located on the Oregon coast.

Service Organizations

American Jewish Joint Distribution Committee | *212/687-6200* | *www.jdc.org* | Also referred to as the Joint, JDC is viewed as a trusted partner that helps propel vulnerable Jewish and non-Jewish communities from dependency to self-sustainability.

B'nai B'rith International | *888/ 388-4224* | *www.bnaibrith.org* | B'nai B'rith International is a national and global leader in the fight against anti-Semitism and anti-Israel bias; provides senior housing and advocacy on issues of vital concern to seniors and their families; helps communities in crisis; and promotes Jewish identity through cultural activities.

National Association of Chevrah Kadisha | *718/847-6280* | *www.nasck.org* | The National Association of Chevra Kadisha, NASCK, was created in order to form a united and cohesive group of Jewish Burial Societies in the United States and Canada. It acts as an umbrella organization to assist affiliated groups in defining, establishing, and achieving the highest degree of traditional Jewish burial practices.

Rotary Club |*847/866-3000* | *www.rotary.org* | Rotary International is the world's first service club organization. Rotary club members are volunteers who work locally, regionally, and internationally to combat hunger, improve health and sanitation, provide education and job training, promote peace, and eradicate polio under the motto "Service Above Self."

Animal-Related Organizations

Guide Dogs for the Blind | *800/295-4050* | *www.guidedogs.com* | Guide Dogs for the Blind provides enhanced mobility to qualified individuals through partnership with dogs whose unique skills are developed and nurtured by dedicated volunteers and a professional staff. Established in 1942, Guide Dogs for the Blind continues its dedication to quality student training services and extensive follow-up support for graduates. Services are provided to students from the United States and Canada at no cost to them.

Humane Society of the United States | *202/452-1100* | *www.humanesociety.org* | The Humane Society of the United States is the nation's largest animal protection organization. They work to reduce suffering and improve the lives of all animals. Their work is done by advocating for better laws and investigating animal cruelty and providing direct care for thousands of animals at emergency shelters, wildlife rehabilitation centers, and mobile veterinary clinics.

Resources for Teachers

Giraffe Project |*360/221-7989* | *www.giraffe.org* | This nonprofit honors the risk-takers, people who are largely unknown, people who have the courage to stick their necks out for the common good, in the United States and around the world. If you are a parent or teacher, perhaps you will be interested in the curriculum available from this nonprofit. In addition, you can browse their giraffe hero database.

Learning to Give | *www.learningtogive.org* | The world's leading developer of lessons and resources that teach giving and volunteerism, civic engagement, and character through service learning.

Acknowledgments

T O MY DISCERNMENT coach, Donna Friedman, thank you for teaching me about figuring in, and living in, possibility. I am grateful for your guidance.

Thanks to the Portland rabbis who were available for advice and help. Thanks especially to Rabbi Brad Greenstein, who answered many questions and pointed me to the right sources to find the answers.

Thank you to Janet Hager, who performed her own mitzvah by helping me with marketing ideas and an awesome logo. Your unwavering belief in me has helped me immensely.

Thanks to Margie Boule for sharing my story in her column in the *Oregonian*.

To Rabbi Leslie and Adina Lipson, for reading my manuscript and offering your suggestions. I am so grateful that our friendship has thrived through the years and despite the miles.

Thanks to Danny Siegel for introducing me to the idea of a mitzvah hero as a teenager. To Arnie Draiman for always being available for support and answers. To Marie Wikle for sharing a common vision and letting me know. To Bonnie Goldberg for lending an ear whenever needed.

Thanks to all the folks in the NSA Oregon chapter. Your confidence and support has bolstered me immensely while this project materialized.

Thank you, to all my friends at Noontime Nomads Toastmasters. You have been an invaluable source of advice and counsel.

243

Rabbi Yonah (z'l) and Lisl Geller, thank you for your friendship, support, and words of wisdom throughout the years.

To my mastermind group: Della Rae, Jennifer Davidson, Juniper Martin, Melissa Peterman, Gigi Rosenburg. Thank you for all your support, encouragement, and sometimes a kick in the pants when I needed it. Thank you for your belief in me during this book adventure! Special thanks to Masterminder Kim Rosenberg, who also read parts of my manuscript and gave me wonderful feedback.

To my literary agent, Deborah Schneider, I know my dad would be smiling at the thought that we collaborated on this book project. Thank you for your guidance and advice throughout the process.

To Krista Lyons, thank you for your confidence in this project and for suggesting the coaching and editing I needed to see it through.

To Brooke Warner, my coach and editor, thank you for your never-ending encouragement and vision. It has been an incredible journey and I have loved every minute of our time working together.

To everyone at Seal Press, especially Merrik Bush-Pirkle. Thank you for answering my never-ending questions with a smile. You have made this book journey an incredible experience.

To all my parents both through birth and marriage—Alayne Rabow, Elaine and Bob Cohen, and Ellen and Allen Pollens. Thank you for your love and enthusiasm in sharing my project with others.

Thank you to my husband, Aaron, whose foresight and intuition envisioned a 1,000 mitzvahs blog. You keep me laughing and help me maintain balance in life. You are my rock and my inspiration. I love you more today than when we met and married eighteen years ago.

To my children, Gabrielle and Solomon, my heart is filled with love and pride for each of you. You both teach me something every day. Solomon, thanks for inspiring me through your actions. Gabrielle, thanks for your endless exuberance for life. Thank you both for keeping me humble. I treasure your presence in my life and I am one very lucky mom!

I want to thank all of my family and friends who have been part of the mitzvah project since it started. Thanks for the emails, notes, and calls of encouragement. Your optimism, expectation, and interest in sharing this project is why this book now exists.

ABOUT THE AUTHOR

L INDA COHEN HOLDS a bachelor's in Jewish Studies from the University of Judaism in Los Angeles (now called the American Jewish University) and a master's from Brandeis University in Jewish Communal Service. She has been both a professional and a lay leader in the Jewish community. She has been an active volunteer since her early thirties, and has participated in untold numbers of volunteer projects. Linda actively encourages people to discover the benefits of being in service to others and living in a state of gratitude.

Linda's children were six and nine years old when the 1,000 mitzvahs project began. The project took two years to complete. Linda lives with her husband, two children, and their dog in Portland, Oregon.

♥ *Visit Linda at www.1000mitzvahs.org.*

SELECTED TITLES FROM SEAL PRESS

For more than thirty years, Seal Press has published groundbreaking books. **By women. For women.**

A Thousand Sisters: My Journey into the Worst Place on Earth to Be a Woman, by Lisa Shannon, foreword by Zainab Salbi. $24.95, 978-1-58005-296-2. Through her inspiring story of turning what started as a solo 30-mile run to raise money for Congolese women into a national organization, Run for Congo Women, Lisa Shannon sounds a deeply moving call to action for each person to find in them the thing that brings meaning to a wounded world.

The Maternal Is Political: Women Writers at the Intersection of Motherhood and Social Change, edited by Shari MacDonald Strong. $15.95, 978-1-58005-243-6. Exploring the vital connection between motherhood and social change, *The Maternal Is Political* features thirty powerful literary essays by women striving to make the world a better place for children and families—both their own and other women's.

A Cluttered Life: Searching for God, Serenity, and My Missing Keys, by Pesi Dinnerstein. $17.00, 978-1-58005-310-5. A chronicle of Pesi Dinnerstein's touching, quirky, and often comic search for order and simplicity amid an onslaught of relentless interruptions.

Run Like a Girl: How Strong Women Make Happy Lives, by Mina Samuels. $16.95, 978-1-58005-345-7. Author and athlete Mina Samuels writes about how lessons learned on the field (or track, or slopes) can help us face challenges in other areas—and how, for many women, participating in sports translates into leading a happier, more fulfilling life.

Travel Therapy: Where Do You Need to Go?, by Karen Schaler. $19.95, 978-1-58005-269-6. Encourages women everywhere to change their attitude by changing their environment.

A Matter of Choice: 25 People Who Transformed Their Lives, edited by Joan Chatfield-Taylor. $14.95, 978-1-58005-118-7. An inspiring collection of essays by people who made profound changes in their work, personal life, location, or lifestyle, proving that it is indeed never too late to take the road less traveled.

Find Seal Press Online
www.SealPress.com
www.Facebook.com/SealPress
Twitter: @SealPress